New Book of
Puzzles

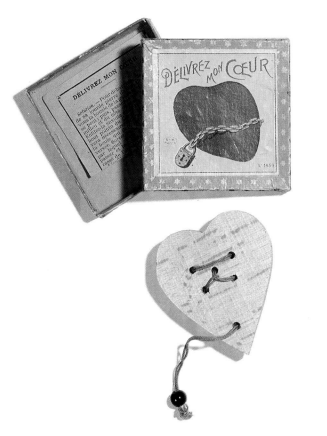

THE GREAT

13
PUZZLE

Something to do — Entirely New
IF YOU CAN DO IT YOU ARE ALL RIGHT,
PATENTED July 25th, 1899

THE IDEA

PRICE

Remove all marbles by jumping
except one [the last one] and it
must land in Centre (Star) Pocket,
it being vacant at the start. This
solves the 13 Puzzle.

WHEN YOU KNOW HOW

PRICE

Yes!
0c

THE ROMAN
PUZZLE

Prove that ha
is either 4
and that half of

What are
made of?

Use 12 BRYANT & MAY'S SWAN VESTAS
IN THE ANSWER.

SWAN
VESTAS

Jerry Slocum and Jack Botermans

New Book of

Puzzles

101 Classic and Modern Puzzles to Make and Solve

Text: Anne Karine Lemstra
Translation: Machteld Cornelissen-Blom, Barbara Eshuis-Clack
Illustrations: Dominique Ampe
Photography: Jack Botermans

W. H. FREEMAN AND COMPANY
New York

ISBN 0 – 7167 – 2356 – 5
Original title: *Puzzels, klassiek en modern.*
Copyright © 1992 by Jack Botermans, Drimmelen, Holland and
Jerry Slocum, Beverly Hills, California.
Puzzles of the collection of Jerry Slocum.
Published by arrangement with Zomer & Keuning Boeken B.V., Ede, Holland.
Distributed in the United States by W. H. Freeman and Company,
41 Madison Avenue, New York, NY 10010.

Compiled by Jack Botermans and Jerry Slocum
Research by Jerry Slocum
Text by Anne Karine Lemstra
Translation by Machteld Cornelissen-Blom and Barbara Eshuis-Clack
Illustrations by Dominique Ampe
Book design and photography by Jack Botermans
Creative organization by Nicolette Botermans

Printed in Hong Kong

1 2 3 4 5 6 7 8 9 0 SS 9 9 8 7 6 5 4 3 2

Library of Congress Cataloging-in-Publication Data

Slocum, Jerry.
    New book of puzzles: 101 classic and modern puzzles to make and
solve / Jerry Slocum, Jack Botermans
        p.   cm.
    Includes bibliographical references (p.) and index.
    ISBN 0-7167-2356-5
    1. Puzzles. I. Botermans, Jack. II. Title.
GV1493. S595   1992
793, 73- -dc20
                                92 - 15918
                                CIP

Contents

Introduction

Vaclav Havel remarked recently that the complexities of life are vast: "There is too much to know… We have to abandon the arrogant belief that the world is merely a puzzle to be solved, a machine with instructions for use waiting to be discovered, a body of information to be fed into a computer." He calls for an increased sense of justice and responsibility; for taste, courage, and compassion.

While reflecting on the wisdom of his words, I couldn't help thinking, "Thank goodness we do also have puzzles that can be solved." I count puzzles among the great pleasures of life, to be enjoyed in moderation like all other treats.

Puzzles add an intellectual dimension to the sensory delights of handling elegantly crafted materials, of colors, shapes and textures and sometimes even smells. Puzzles help us exercise our gray cells and sharpen our wits, because they often clarify points that are confusing in more complicated contexts.

When my wife and I have invited small groups of college students to our home in an attempt to get to know them better, we've learned that it is wise to set a dozen or so puzzles out in the room. Nothing else breaks ice as well. (But I can't risk treating all my puzzles this way – I can do it only with puzzles for which I know enough theory to put them back together again after they've been arbitrarily rearranged.)

Jerry Slocum's puzzle collection is legendary, and in 1986 he joined forces with Jack Botermans to publish a magnificent book entitled *Puzzles Old and New*. The closing paragraph in Martin Gardner's introduction to that book observed that "New mechanical puzzles are being invented every year and it will not be long before this elegant volume will be in need of updating." The present book, a worthy successor to the first, fulfills that prediction while giving us an even better window on historical developments.

My own interest in this subject is amplified by strong connections between puzzles and algorithms. The authors tell us how to build many of the puzzles from bits of wood, paper, metal, and string; but I am sure that many readers will actually enjoy "fabricating" them from bits and bytes inside a computer. Exciting advances toward "virtual reality" are now being made, so that programmers can capture the visual and even tactile pleasures of puzzle manipulation as well as the purely logical delights that our machines had in previous decades.

Happy puzzling to all, as we move into an exhilarating new age with a deeper appreciation of the glorious past!

Donald E. Knuth

TANGRAM

The Tangram puzzle is undoubtedly one of the best known of all the mechanical puzzles. Seven geometrical shapes, the tans (five triangles, one square and one parallelogram), together form a square. The puzzle is to arrange these pieces to form a problem figure. It is its simplicity that makes it so fascinating a puzzle and at the same time so difficult to solve. That is why this type of dissection puzzle has been a brain-teaser for many centuries.

Tangram originated in China where it has been around for centuries. The Chinese call it Ch'i Ch'io. In the eighteenth century, during the rule of emperor Chia Ch'ing (1796 – 1820), Tangram books were printed for the first time. In these books all kinds of examples of Tangram problems were shown.

In the early nineteenth century the puzzle found its way to Europe and America. It became very popular. The first European publication dates from as early as 1805. Even Napoleon, exiled on St. Helena, is said to have been an avid Tangram player.

Sam Loyd started a Tangram myth. Loyd, in *The 8th Book of Tan*, suggested that the puzzle was invented four thousand years earlier by the God Tan and described in the *7 Books of Tan*. And Loyd himself compiled no fewer than 600 problems. Since then the popularity of the puzzle has not faded, and it has gained as strong a foothold in the West as it has in the East.

1.

Put-together puzzles.
Objective: Putting the pieces together is the puzzle.
Pages 8–37

The 8th Book of Tan, a book with over 600 Tangram problems that Sam Loyd published in 1903. The price was one dollar and schools were especially keen buyers.

The diagram shows how a square can be divided into seven pieces to make a Tangram puzzle.

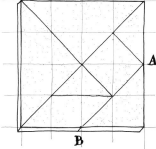

HOW TO MAKE YOUR OWN TANGRAM PUZZLE

All you need to make your own Tangram puzzle is a piece of 4 x 4 in. (10 x 10 cm) plywood. Two diagonals divide the square into four triangles. Connect the middle point of side A with that of side B. The small triangle in the upper righthand corner is made by drawing a line parallel to the diagonal, and the parallelogram at the bottom is made by drawing a line parallel to the bottom. You then saw out the pieces along the lines with a fret saw. Sandpaper the pieces until nice and smooth. Apply a coat of varnish or paint for the finishing touch.

HOW TO SOLVE TANGRAM PUZZLES

There are several ways to use the Tangram pieces. First, without a solution, you try to put the square back together again. Then you can try and arrange the seven pieces into the problems shown on this page. Or you can have a go at finding new problems yourself. Trace the outline of a new figure on a piece of paper and see if your friends can find the solution. Therefore, Tangram makes a good competitive game.

Chinesisches Geduldspiel. On the trade cards for Voelcker's chicory coffee extract were pictures of Tangram figures. These early twentieth century lithographs reflect the puzzle's popularity with people of all ages.

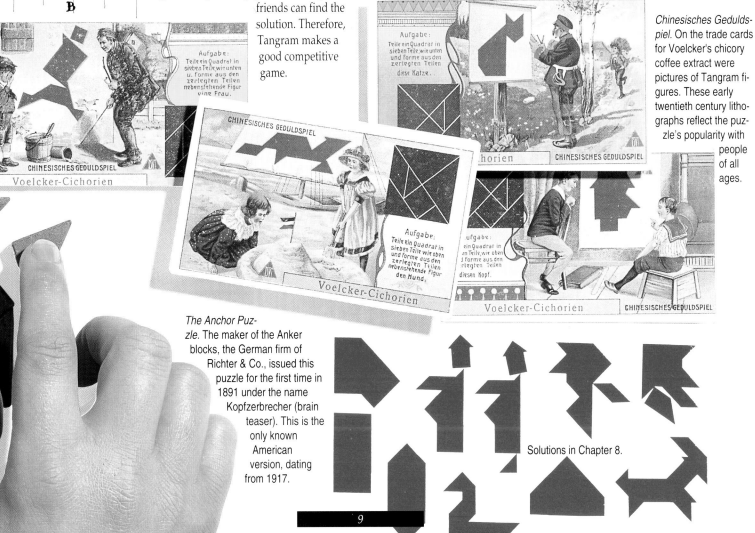

The Anchor Puzzle. The maker of the Anker blocks, the German firm of Richter & Co., issued this puzzle for the first time in 1891 under the name Kopfzerbrecher (brain teaser). This is the only known American version, dating from 1917.

Solutions in Chapter 8.

JIGSAW PUZZLES

Around the year 1760, the Englishman John Spilsbury made the first jigsaw puzzle. He mounted maps on thin panels of mahogany and sawed them into segments. These puzzles were intended as educational toys; by piecing the maps together children would learn without effort what the world looked like. Now there are jigsaw puzzles that have from four to several thousand pieces, with pictures of works of art to children's drawings. The variety is so vast that, with the exception of one example, we will not go into jigsaw puzzles here. However, we did not want to leave out one jigsaw puzzle as this is the most beautiful one we ever found: a map of the United States segmented into puzzle pieces.

Dissected Map of the United States: This map of the United States as a jigsaw puzzle was marketed in 1887 by the New York firm of McLoughlin Bros.

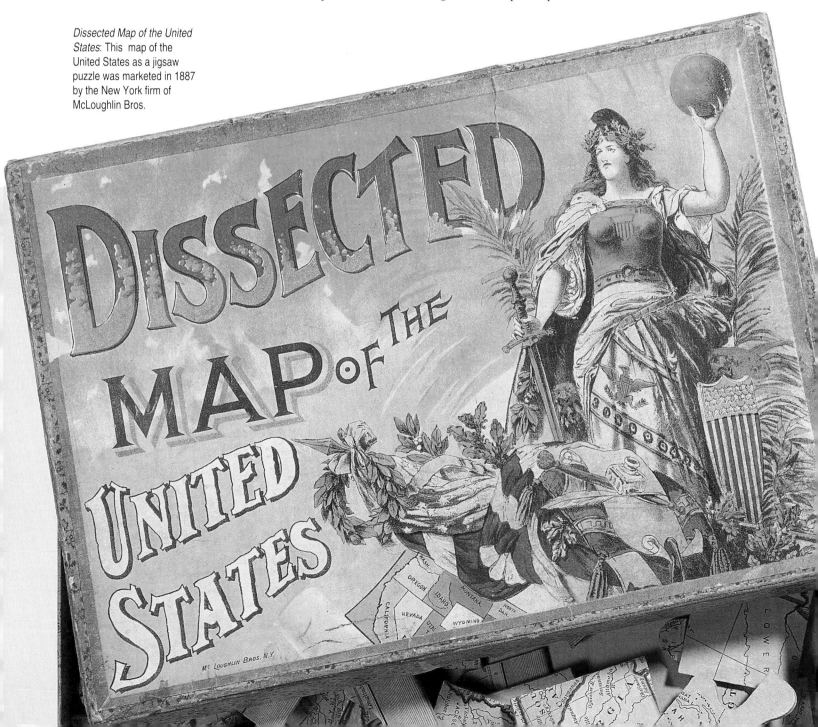

HOW TO MAKE YOUR OWN JIGSAW PUZZLE

The easy way is for you to take a photograph to a photo print shop where they will enlarge it for you and stamp out the puzzle pieces. We think it is more fun to make one yourself.

Take, for instance, a map of a country or the street plan of the place where you live and mount it on a piece of thin plywood. On the back of the plywood draw the pattern given in this book. Using the grid you can make the pattern any size you wish. Of course you can also make different patterns. Use your imagination. Next you saw out the pieces.

Suggestion: Before you start sawing, clamp a piece of cardboard or plywood to the map side of the puzzle. This will keep the wood from splintering and keep the edges of the map neat. Finish the puzzle with varnish and it will last longer.

If you want to make a very large puzzle with many pieces, simply use the pattern as many times as necessary, taking care that the pieces correspond exactly! This can be done by overlapping the edges of the pattern by approximately 5⁄8 in. (1.5 cm).

Left: You see the pattern of the puzzle pieces. By using them side by side and one above the other you can make any size puzzle. Make sure that the pieces correspond exactly on all sides!

LETTER PUZZLES

Letters, of course, are ideal objects for making puzzles. They have long been a popular way of advertising. The puzzles would have printed advertisements for certain brands and would be distributed among the customers. Of these puzzles, the best known is undoubtedly the T-puzzle. In spite of the fact that it had only four pieces, it was very difficult. The initials of famous people were also used for puzzles, for instance, the F D Puzzle, named after Franklin Delano Roosevelt, the 35th president of the United States. Oblong-shaped letters, such as the L and the Z, are the most suitable for letter puzzles. Examples of these are the New L-Square Puzzle and the Squares and Oblong Puzzles shown here.

The T-Puzzle. The earliest known example was an advertisement for White Rose Ceylon Tea dating from 1903. The firm of Armour & Co. advertised their sausages with a puzzle, also known as the Teaser.

Solutions in Chapter 8.

The F D Puzzle – World Famous Initials. Franklin D. Roosevelt's initials were made into a puzzle by the Perry & Elliot Co. in 1933, the first year that he was in office. The F consisted of 5 red pieces, the D of 6 blue pieces. One of the blue pieces in the photograph is missing.

HOW TO MAKE YOUR OWN LETTER PUZZLE

The pieces of the puzzles on this page are given separately in the diagram. The puzzle is best made of birch plywood, about 1/8 in. (2 mm) thick. It is expensive but very durable. Trace the outlines of the pieces on the plywood and saw them out with a fine-toothed fret saw. Next you sandpaper the edges and finish the pieces with matte varnish.

Of course it is more of a challenge to make a puzzle from your own initials. Always draw rectangular letters, because round shapes will make the puzzle too easy. The stroke-width of the letter should be approximately 3/4 in. (2 cm) in all places. To make the puzzle more difficult, divide the letter in as few pieces as possible and at a diagonal angle. First make your design of paper and have somebody solve it. Make sure it is really difficult before you make it of wood. Puzzle initials also make nice gifts.

The New L-Square Puzzle. In 1915, F. O. Degenhardt of New York patented a puzzle consisting of nine L-shaped pieces stamped out of sheet metal together forming a square. It was a variation of the 1807 Bestelmeier puzzle.

Below: Diagram in which the proportions of the three puzzles on this page are shown.

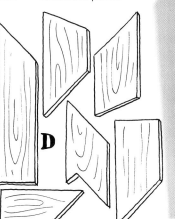

F

D

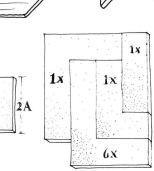

2A

A

2A

1x

1x

1x

2A

6x

Solutions in Chapter 8.

Right: *Squares & Oblongs Puzzles.* These puzzles from England consisted of 8 L- and Z-shaped pieces together forming an oblong or a square.

SQUARE DISSECTION PUZZLES

Cut a square piece of cardboard into a number of equal-sized pieces, then cut some of these again in two, and you will have an instant puzzle. Try to make it difficult with a dozen or fewer pieces.

A good example of a difficult puzzle of this type is shown here, from the soup and sauce manufacturer T. A. Snider. This Diamond Puzzle consisted of ten pieces which form a square. The pieces are either triangles or parallelograms, which doesn't make it any easier.

The Diamond Puzzle was distributed for advertising purposes. The consumer solving the puzzle would get a good look at the T. A. Snider products, since each puzzle piece had a picture of one of their products on it.

The Diamond Puzzle from T. A. Snider Preserve Co. of Ohio was used for advertising. However, the basic puzzle is much older, and was shown in the Bestelmeier Toy Catalog of 1803 under the name of Five squares make One.

The diagram shows the shape of the puzzle. It is essential that you cut the puzzle precisely or it will not fit together properly.

Solutions in Chapter 8.

HOW TO MAKE THIS PUZZLE

In this case we start from a diamond shape to make the pieces, and we keep up the suspense by not giving away the solution at once. For the end result should be a square! Make the pieces from plywood or cardboard as shown in the diagram. Using the grid will enable you to enlarge the puzzle. Then divide the large shape into six equal parallelograms. Cut two of these parallelograms in half and cut the triangles from the other two. Make sure to cut the corners carefully, or else the puzzle won't fit together properly. You can decorate the puzzle to your own taste.

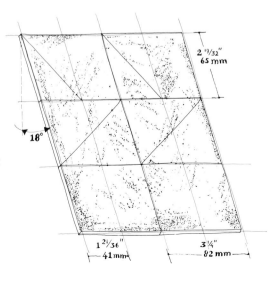

A MAGIC PUZZLE

A magic puzzle? Try it and you will see that solving it isn't simple. The photo shows the Fresh Milk Puzzle. It was put out by the National Milk Publicity Council, presumably in the thirties, to promote the drinking of more milk. The idea behind it was: a healthy body with fresh milk, and a healthy mind with a difficult puzzle.

The card had to be cut along the lines into six strips. These then had to be arranged to form the word MILK. No folding the pieces! Like we said: "a very tricky puzzle"!

The Fresh Milk Puzzle was put out by the National Milk Council. As far as we know it was the first puzzle of this kind. Several versions have appeared recently in books and Christmas cards.

HOW TO MAKE THE MAGIC PUZZLE

Take a piece of 4 3⁄4 x 2 3⁄8 in. (12 x 6 cm) heavy paper. Divide it into six strips, each 4 3⁄4 in. (2 cm)wide and 2 3⁄8 in. (6 cm) long. (Alas! Now we have to give away the secret for you to make the puzzle.) Braid the strips into a square, as in the diagram. Write the word MILK or your name on one side of the braided square. Make bold and legible letters. If you wish to make it more complicated, write a different word or name in a different color on the other side. Undo the braiding and you have your "puzzle"! Now see if you can put it together again. You know the solution and yet . . .

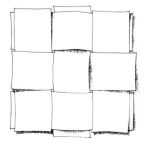

SOLUTION
This diagram shows the solution to the puzzle. You need it to make the puzzle and, perhaps, to solve it!

THE ENDLESS CHAIN

This French puzzle from the end of the last century is a put-together puzzle with an added design feature.
The puzzle is to form a square with the eighteen pieces with the chain connected into a continuous loop.
There are many ways to fit the pieces into a square, but making a continuous chain makes it a difficult puzzle.
When you have found a new solution, write it down. Then see if someone else can solve it your way.
This Chaine sans Fin can also be used to play a domino game. Deal the pieces with the chain on them. Each
player takes one piece, and the one who holds the piece with the most links on it begins.
You play by trying to match a piece with the previously played one.
The first player to have used up all of his or her pieces is the winner.

SOLUTION
The diagram shows how the
square is divided into rectan-
gles and how the chain winds
across them.

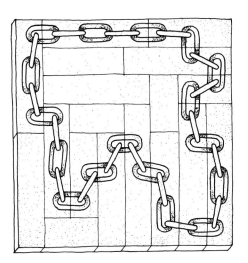

When you have cut all the
pieces, you will find out the
difficulty of this puzzle.

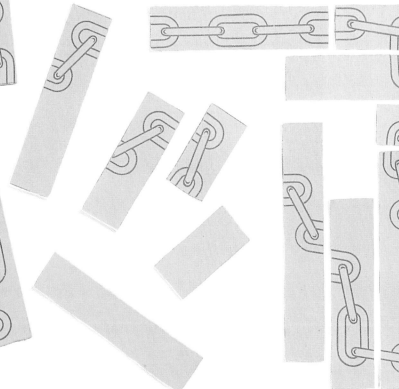

HOW TO MAKE THE CHAIN PUZZLE

Take a 6 1/4 x 6 1/4 in. (16 x 16 cm) piece of cardboard. On this you draw 64 (8 x 8) squares of 3/4 x 3/4 in. (2 x 2 cm) each. The diagram shows the lines along which you cut. Mark these clearly on the cardboard with a color by using the squares you have drawn. This will prevent you from making the wrong cuts. You now have 18 different pieces. Copy the drawing of the chain on the board. You could also draw a rope, but a chain makes the puzzle more difficult. Cut out the 18 pieces, and your puzzle is ready. A fancier version can be made of plywood.

A very interesting variation is made by using a real iron chain. The puzzle can be made from the chain with the links welded or glued together. Buy a 34-link piece of chain. Arrange it in the same pattern as shown in the diagram, after you have enlarged it to the correct size using the grid. Then glue or weld the links according to the pattern in the diagram. If you use a special glue it will be almost as strong as if it was welded. Then saw the chain in those places where, in the diagram, the edges of the rectangle are shown. File the rough edges smooth, and your puzzle is complete. Maybe you can think up new variations of this puzzle.

La Chaine Sans Fin was put out by publisher Simonin-Cuny in Paris before 1893. It was a true "casse-tête" because of its difficulty. Not only do the pieces have to form a square, but in addition the chain has to form a continuous loop.

An attractive version is to use an actual iron chain for the puzzle, ranging from tiny links to a kind of giant puzzle. The links can be glued or welded together.

MAGIC SQUARES

According to legend, four thousand years ago, in China, there lived the emperor Yu.
One day, while strolling along the Yellow River, he saw a tortoise whose shell was patterned in squares.
Each square contained a number of dots. Upon taking a closer look at the creature, he
discovered that the sum of each row of dots, whether across, down or diagonally, was the same. The tortoise
became a court legend. Great significance was attributed to the series of numbers, which were called Lo Shu.
They soon appeared on amulets and magic stones. In China, the even numbers of the Lo Shu are equated
with Yin (the feminine force in the universe), and the odd numbers with Yang
(the masculine force in the universe).
Lo Shu is the only magic square of the third order, i.e. the square contains 3 x 3 cells (a total of 9). The sum of
the numbers in each row, across, down and diagonally, is 15. This number is also called the constant. There
are also magic squares of a higher order which offer a multitude of possibilities– for instance, 880 squares of
the fourth order (4 x 4), and several million of the fifth order. So you see there is an incredible variation on
the original magic square. One example is the Giant Puzzle.

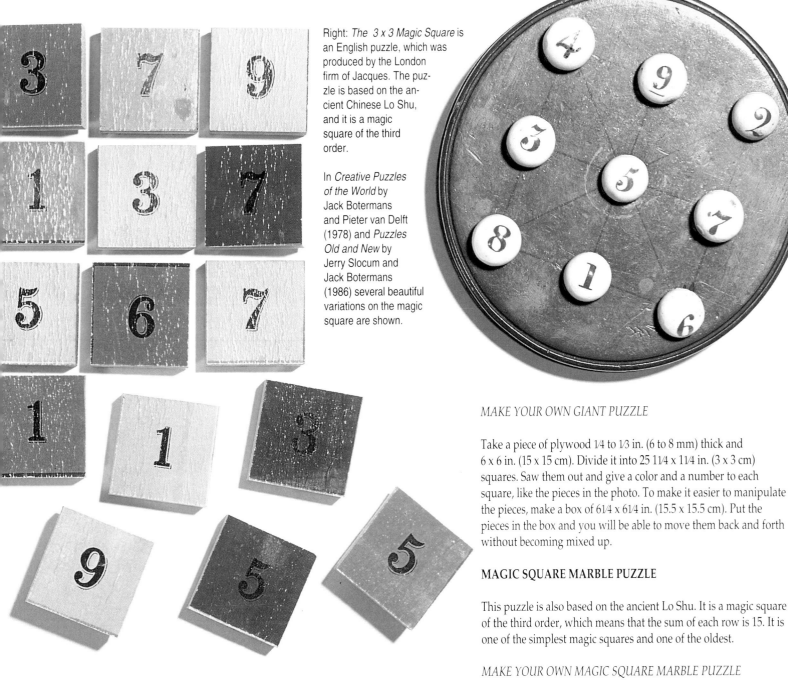

Right: *The 3 x 3 Magic Square* is an English puzzle, which was produced by the London firm of Jacques. The puzzle is based on the ancient Chinese Lo Shu, and it is a magic square of the third order.

In *Creative Puzzles of the World* by Jack Botermans and Pieter van Delft (1978) and *Puzzles Old and New* by Jerry Slocum and Jack Botermans (1986) several beautiful variations on the magic square are shown.

The Giant Puzzle was produced by McLoughlin Bros. of New York in 1888. At that time they were one of the largest game and puzzle manufacturers in America.

Solutions in Chapter 8.

THE GIANT PUZZLE

The McLoughlin Bros. Giant Puzzle is a magic square of the fifth order (5 x 5 cells). The numbered blocks must be arranged in a square in such a way that neither vertically, horizontally or diagonally the same numbers appear in one row. Neither should the same color more than once appear in one row. And finally, the sum of each row, whether across, down or diagonally, must be 25. The puzzle is easy to make but oh so hard to solve.

MAKE YOUR OWN GIANT PUZZLE

Take a piece of plywood 1/4 to 1/3 in. (6 to 8 mm) thick and 6 x 6 in. (15 x 15 cm). Divide it into 25 1 1/4 x 1 1/4 in. (3 x 3 cm) squares. Saw them out and give a color and a number to each square, like the pieces in the photo. To make it easier to manipulate the pieces, make a box of 6 1/4 x 6 1/4 in. (15.5 x 15.5 cm). Put the pieces in the box and you will be able to move them back and forth without becoming mixed up.

MAGIC SQUARE MARBLE PUZZLE

This puzzle is also based on the ancient Lo Shu. It is a magic square of the third order, which means that the sum of each row is 15. It is one of the simplest magic squares and one of the oldest.

MAKE YOUR OWN MAGIC SQUARE MARBLE PUZZLE

Take a piece of wood, 5 1/8 x 5 1/8 in. (13 x 13 cm) by 1/2 in. (1 cm) thick. Saw out a circle with a 5 1/8 in. (13 cm) diameter. Around the central point mark the nine spots in a square pattern. Drill holes for the marbles. Note: only bore the tip of the drill a bit into the wood to create a small conical hole which can hold the marble. Smooth the board using medium sandpaper. Using a black felt-tip pen draw the lines linking the holes. Now all you have to do is find nine white marbles and mark them 1 to 9. To preserve the numbers and lines, varnish the marbles and the board.

ANIMAL PUZZLES

Animals are a favorite subject for puzzles. Take for example the puzzle of the two tired dogs that magically become two running dogs simply by adding a few lines.

Such a puzzle is no novelty though.

The idea of two figures which have four halves that are interchangeable dates back to the Middle Ages. The Cathedral of Rouen's Portail des Librairies has a relief from 1290–1300 portraying two men that can be viewed horizontally as well as vertically to see four figures.

In the nineteenth century this idea was rediscovered by several puzzle designers. In an 1867 periodical there is a puzzle illustration of two horses and jockeys. At first glance they look like two tired horses with hunched backs. If you look at them more closely and give them a quarter turn, they come to life at a full gallop.

In 1871, Sam Loyd, later named "the prince of puzzle designers," developed his Trick Donkeys using the same principle. He cut the picture into three pieces, two with donkeys and a strip with two jockeys. These were to be arranged to make the two jockeys mounted on the donkeys. The puzzle was a huge success and Loyd made $10,000 in just a few weeks. In the years to follow, Loyd's Trick Donkeys remained very popular. They were used for advertising and even as one company's trademark. Later, Loyd created many other world-famous puzzles. The idea of the Trick Donkeys was used by many other puzzle designers to make new animal puzzles, often for advertising products.

The Donkey Puzzle served as advertising for shoe manufacturer Standard Screw. It's almost identical to Sam Loyd's original Trick Donkeys. The puzzle came in an envelope bearing an ad for Standard Screw shoes, and it cautioned the consumer not to buy imitations!

Solutions in Chapter 8.

HOW TO MAKE YOUR OWN ANIMAL PUZZLE

Left: *The Animated Dogs* by the R. D. Housden-Puzzle Adv. Co. of New York were based on the same principle as the Trick Donkeys of Loyd's. This puzzle advertised Dr. Walker's Vinegar Bitters, a remedy for sundry ailments. The task set by the puzzle was to transform the two listless dogs into active ones, without folding the card, just as Dr. Walker's Bitters turned listless people into active people.

On these pages you see a number of animal puzzles, all based on Loyd's donkey puzzle. There were cats with witches and dogs. Some of them were with boxes, some of them without. Most of these were used for advertising purposes in the late nineteenth century.

The easiest way to make your own animal puzzle is by tracing one of the examples onto transparent paper and gluing it onto a piece of cardboard. If you trace the lines on the transparent paper with pastel or charcoal, you can then transfer the drawing to paper or cardboard. You can also draw a copy of one of the examples yourself. Color it in nicely and glue it on plywood or cardboard. You may want to give it a protective coat of varnish.

Les Deux Mulets is almost an exact copy of Sam Loyd's Trick Donkeys. The puzzle was produced in France by V.-W. et Cie. and came in a pretty box with a color lithograph of two obstinate mules and their riders.

The Witches Puzzle, 1938, was a puzzle advertising Dickinson's Witch Hazel, produced by Walker Rackliff. Witch hazel was used as a disinfectant for cuts suffered while shaving. The back of the puzzle proclaimed that this lotion was the best. The puzzle is a variation of Sam Loyd's Trick Donkeys. Obviously, the title of the puzzle refers to the name of the product.

21

AFTER ANIMALS CAME PEOPLE

In 1871 many imitations of the Sam Loyd's Trick Donkey puzzle appeared on the market. Scores of animal puzzles appeared. One example thereof is the French animal puzzle Bucephale, shown here. This puzzle is based on Sam Loyd's pony puzzle of 1861–1865. During the American Civil War, Loyd went to Europe to sell United States Bonds. On his way back, he learned about the "White Horse of Uffington Hill" (Berkshire, England). This mysterious figure inspired the Governor of Pennsylvania to suggest that this might be a wonderful subject for a puzzle. After several minutes Loyd produced the Pony Puzzle, a black horse cut into 6 pieces. These were to be rearranged to make a new horse. It became one of Loyd's most successful puzzles. For this puzzle, the solution was not in the pieces themselves, but in the silhouette that you can make with the six pieces. Based on both this and the braided puzzle on p. 15, a number of new put-together puzzles are shown that use

"Les Quatre Vagabonds" was of German origin and was shown in Hoffmann's *Puzzles Old and New* in 1893. This version was produced by the firm of Les Jeux et Jouets Francais.

animal rather than human images. The object is to create a new image by covering parts of the puzzle pieces. Thus, four funny little men become one. Four boxers also turn out to be just one, and thunderclouds are not what they appear to be at first.

The Willard-Johnson Prize Fight Puzzle was based on the 1915 boxing match between Jack Johnson, heavyweight champion of 1908, and Jess Willard. Willard won the match and held the title until 1919. The puzzle was produced by the Magic Shop of Philadelphia.

Bucephale was produced by G. B. et C. N. K. Atlas of Paris after 1925. It was based on Sam Loyd's Pony Puzzle.

Below: On this grid you can see the outline of the horse.

HOW TO MAKE A BUCEPHALE PUZZLE

Plywood is suitable for making a Bucephale puzzle. On the grid you can see the outline of the horse. Copy this onto a 4 x 6 in. (10 x 15 cm) piece of plywood. Saw along the lines and sandpaper the pieces. You may want to paint or lacquer the pieces to finish the job nicely.
We recommend you make a box of 5 1/2 x 2 3/8 x 1/2 in. (14 x 6 x 1 cm) to store the pieces.
If you would like to have the other puzzles, copy them and glue them to cardboard. But why not use your own imagination and make your own version? For Les Quatre Vagabonds as well as Un Sage dans les Nuages and the Boxer the proportions of the pieces are 1 : 2.

SOLUTIONS

To make the puzzle, we have to show the solution with every puzzle.

Un Sage dans les Nuages: this philosophical puzzle was put on the market by Les Jeux et Jouets Francais (Paris) between 1904 and 1930. The face of the sage Socrates is hidden in the clouds.

EDGE MATCHING PUZZLES

In America these puzzles are known as edge matching puzzles. The puzzle is to match colors, numbers or images at the edges where the puzzle pieces touch each other. The Pair-it Puzzle consists of seven hexagons. These must be arranged in the circle in the box so that all the touching sides have the same numbers. To this puzzle there is just one solution, and it was not included with the puzzle but had to be bought separately for 10 cents in the shop where the puzzle was purchased.

The other puzzle, l'Arc en Ciel, works the other way around. Nine circles with four colored stars must be turned in such a way that the six colors get correctly distributed in a horizontal as well as a perpendicular direction. The same colors cannot touch each other, nor can the same color combinations occur twice. When in a horizontal row blue and red touch, they cannot touch in another horizontal row. The same rules apply for the columns also.

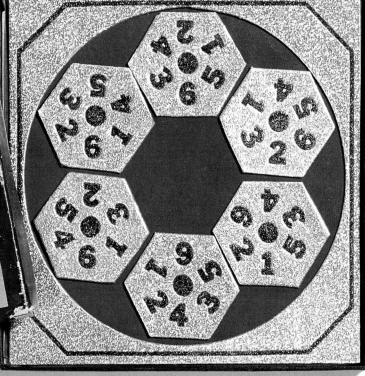

The Pair-it Puzzle by the Douglas Novelty Co. of Michigan. This example has the seventh hexagon missing.

HOW TO MAKE AN EDGE MATCHING PUZZLE

For making the Pair-it Puzzle you need a 4 3⁄4 x 4 3⁄4 in. (12 x 12 cm) piece of cardboard or plywood. Trace the diagram on this page or draw it by using the grid. The grid will enable you to make it any size you want. Cut or saw out the hexagons. When you use plywood, sand the edges of the pieces before going on. Next, put the numbers on the pieces. Follow the example accurately, otherwise the puzzle may be unsolvable. You can use a felt-tip pen or brush and paint, but rub-on numbers will give a better result, and look very professional. If you use rub-on numbers, the pieces should be varnished because they damage easily. You can also go to a hardware store and buy seven large hex nuts on which you paint or rub on the numbers. Varnish them and your puzzle is ready.

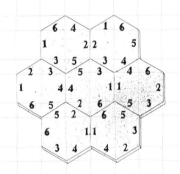

The pattern for the hexagons of the Pair-it Puzzle. Using the grid they can be made in- to any size. This pattern also gives the solution to the puzzle.

The *l'Arc en Ciel* puzzle by V-W. et Cie. of France consisted of nine wooden disks attached to the bottom of the box by pegs, enabling them to rotate without shifting.

SOLUTIONS
The diagram and the photo show the solutions to these puzzles.

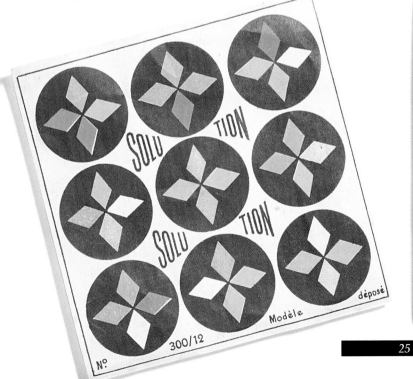

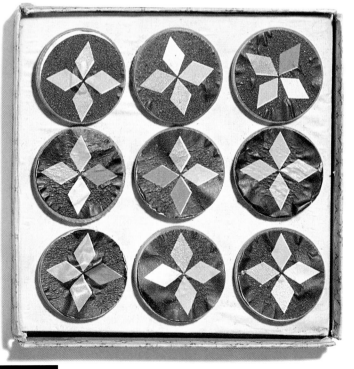

The seven pieces of 4 nuts each make a tough puzzle.

The Hexagone was designed by Peer Clausen and is produced by the Swiss firm of Spiel Naef. A folding card containing many problems comes with the puzzle.

A PUZZLE MADE USING NUTS

In general nuts are used to attach one thing to another. But a nut is also an ideal object for fixing your mind. The puzzle on this page is made of nuts and belongs to the polyform family. Polyforms are different groups of similar shapes, in this case hexagons, which can be combined into larger shapes.

In this Swiss puzzle, the Hexagone, the seven pieces of 4 nuts each make a tough puzzle. The pieces represent all the planar figures that can be made of 4 identical hexagons. See if you can find the solutions to the problem on this page.

The special "super glue" should be handled with great care or before you know it your fingers will be firmly stuck together. A tiny drop of glue will be enough.

Solutions in Chapter 8.

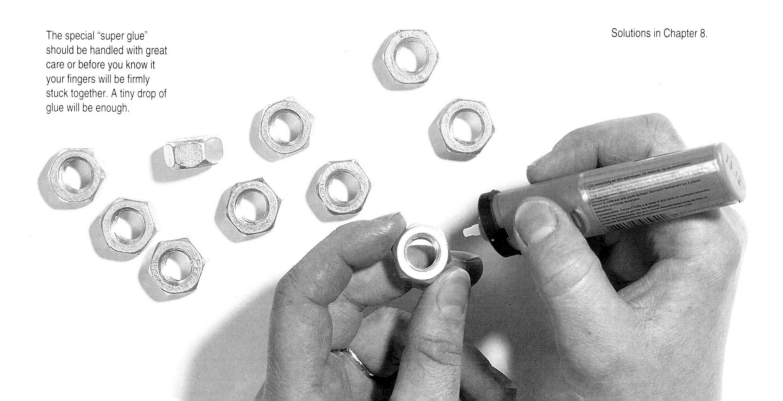

THE NUT PYRAMID

This puzzle is based on the use of hex nuts. The pieces are shown below: one of 2, four of 3, four of 4, and one of 5 nuts. When glued together neatly and precisely they form a pyramid with a triangular base with sides of 5 nuts and a height of 5 nuts.

This very difficult Nut-Pyramistory was put on the market in Japan by Adult-Thinking Games. After we photographed it, it took us half an hour to put the puzzle back together again!

HOW TO MAKE THESE NUT PUZZLES

All you need is 7 x 4 = 28 nuts for the Hexagone and 35 nuts for the pyramid and a tube of super glue suitable for metal. On these pages you can see exactly how the nuts should be glued together. A tiny bit of glue on each surface is sufficient.

Note: when you are gluing two nuts together, put adjacent nuts in their correct places against the nuts being glued to prevent them from not fitting later on. Start by gluing 4 nuts in a straight line. Use this as a guide to make the other shapes.

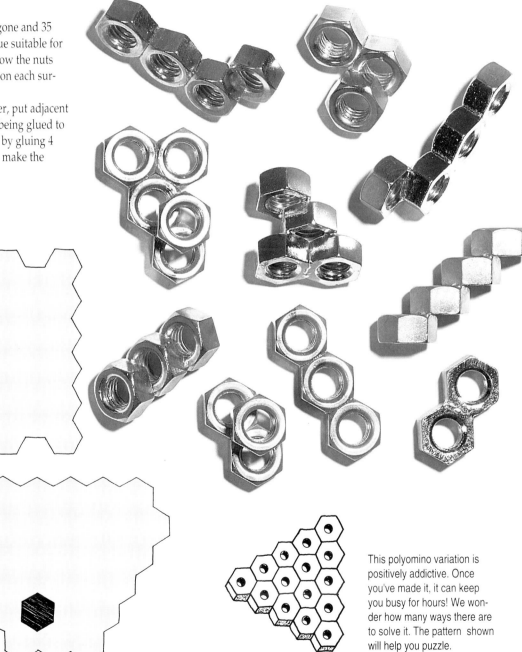

These puzzle problems can be solved with the seven pieces of the Hexagone. When you have found one solution, write it down and explore other solutions for the same problem.

This polyomino variation is positively addictive. Once you've made it, it can keep you busy for hours! We wonder how many ways there are to solve it. The pattern shown will help you puzzle.

MAGIC NUMBERS

Countless puzzles have been designed and made based on numbers. Remember the magic squares. For these puzzles you will have to take your time. People with a gift for math will especially enjoy the three puzzles based on the ordering of numbers.

These puzzles too can easily be made of wood or cardboard, but they are very hard to solve! The basic principle is to turn the numbered pieces so as to provide the correct arithmetic sum. The outcome, in each case, is given. You just need to arrange the pieces so that the total is correct on all sides.

THE WASHINGTON MOMUMENT PUZZLE

This puzzle, in the shape of the Washington Monument, has ten wooden blocks with numbers on four sides. These numbers should add to a total of 555 on each side. The blocks must be turned to reach the correct total on all four sides.

The White Shoe Store of Providence put the puzzle on the market and promised a reward to the first person to send in the right solution. The reward was $500 worth of shoes, which, in the thirties, amounted to a small fortune!

HOW TO MAKE A MONUMENT PUZZLE

The easiest way is to use 10 building blocks of uniform size. You could also saw 10 cubes from a 1 x 1 in. (2.5 x 2.5 cm) piece of wood of 10 1/4 in. (26 cm) long (1/2 in. (1 cm) extra for loss through sawing). Drill a 1/8 in. (3 mm) hole through the exact center of the blocks, taking care that all the holes match when stacking the blocks. The diagram shows you how to put the numbers on the blocks. Follow these instructions exactly, or the puzzle may not work. Next, make a base of wood. Drill a hole in the center and glue in a dowel of 1/8 in. (2.5 mm) diameter and 10 5/8 in. (27 cm) high. Slide the blocks over the peg and put a decorative piece of wood on top.

Solutions in Chapter 8.

This diagram shows the locations of the numbers to be used in the puzzle. It is essential to copy them accurately.

60	95	30	25
55	25	20	70
20	50	55	10
65	15	45	55
90	55	90	80
90	85	55	60
55	45	95	15
55	55	75	65
35	55	55	70
55	55	60	75

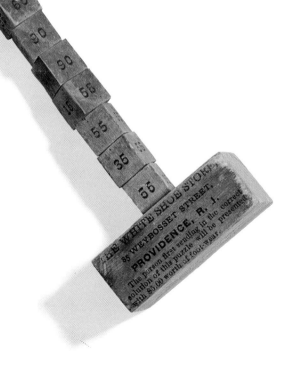

The Washington Monument Puzzle was put on the market by Hampton Toy Co. of Massachusetts. It was based on the Washington Monument, designed in 1848 and opened in 1888. It is an obelisk with an overall height of 555 feet. The number 555 is also the total of each side of the puzzle when it is solved.

Above: *The Hegger Revolving Century Puzzle* was used for advertising for Imperial "Hygienique Fluid". On the back of the puzzle was the firm's ad. However, the puzzle had to be purchased for 5 cents.

Right: *The Safe Combination Puzzle* appeared in 1891. It was devised by a safe specialist and the solution was the combination to the safe of a major bank! An ideal puzzle for would-be bank robbers!

THE WHO BROKE THE BANK PUZZLE

Making this puzzle is even easier, but the solution is not at all easy. Three square pieces of cardboard are marked with numbers that, when rotated to the proper position, simultaneously add up to 40 in eight places. The manufacturer of this puzzle was a renowned safe expert, and the solution to the puzzle was alleged to be the same as the combination to the safe of one of America's largest banks. Amazing,

how a
5-cent puzzle can
make you feel so ineffective.

HOW TO MAKE YOUR OWN BANK PUZZLE

Cut three cardboard squares of 3 1⁄8, x 3 1⁄8, 2 3⁄8 x 2 3⁄8, and 1 5⁄8 x 1 5⁄8 in. (8 x 8, 6 x 6, and 4 x 4 cm). Copy the numbers from the example exactly on your own puzzle. Attach them to a base with a cotter pin through the center. Use different-colored cardboard for each square to provide a colorful puzzle. You can color or decorate them as you like.

THE REVOLVING CENTURY PUZZLE

This Revolving Century Puzzle was put on the market in 1910 as advertising by a manufacturer of liquid disinfectants. The principle is similar to that of the Monument Puzzle. Here, the blocks have been replaced by cardboard disks, which rotate. The task is to turn the disks to make the numbers on all six columns add up to a total of 100 each. Very hard to do.

HOW TO MAKE THE REVOLVING CENTURY PUZZLE

SOLUTIONS
The Who Broke The Bank Puzzle and The Revolving Century Puzzle you have to solve yourself.

Cut six cardboard circles with diameters of 4, 3 1⁄2, 3 1⁄8, 2 3⁄4, 2 3⁄8, and 2 in.(10, 9, 8, 7, 6, and 5 cm) respectively. For the base you need a square piece of cardboard of 6 x 6 in. (15 x 15 cm) and a cotter pin. Put the numbers on the circles as shown on the example. Be precise. Make a hole in the center of each circle and mount them on the square base with the cotter pin. You can color or decorate the puzzle to your own liking.

THE 25 Y PUZZLE

This cube is entirely built up of 25 identical puzzle pieces, the Y. This Y is one of the 12 pentominoes, a form which is composed of five cubes. Penta means five; the Pentagon is a five-sided building. The shapes of pentominoes resemble letters of the alphabet and have been named after them. The puzzle is made by assembling a cube from the 25 Y's. That is quite a task, because the eventual cube is only 2½ x 2½ x 2½ in. (5 x 5 x 5 cm)! How to fit 25 pieces into such a small object?!

The solution is pictured on the box in which the puzzle comes– very fortunate for the puzzlers who would otherwise never be able to get the pieces back in the box.

The puzzle was discovered by David Klarner and published by him and C. J. Bouwkamp in an article in 1970 in the *Journal of Recreational Mathematics*. In addition to the puzzle of 25 Y's filling a 2 x 2 x 2 in. (5 x 5 x 5 cm) box exactly, David Klarner tells us that 10 y's will fill a ½ x 2 x 4 in.(1 x 5 x 10 cm) box, 12 Y's will fill a ¾ x 2 x 2 ⅜ in. (2 x 5 x 6 cm) box and a 1 ¼ x 1 ⅝ x 2 in. (3 x 4 x 5 cm) box, 16 Y's will fill a 1 ⅝ x 1 ⅝ x 2 in. (4 x 4 x 5 cm) box and 20 will fill a 1 ⅝ x 2 x 2 in. (4 x 5 x 5 cm) box.

Your Y pentominoes can be used for all these puzzles, some of which are fairly easy and some are very difficult. We will leave it to you to find out which is which.

These 25 Y-pieces are pentominoes. They are forms that consist of five identical cubes. Together these 25 Y's can be assembled into one cube.

HOW TO MAKE THE 25 Y's

The dimensions of the pieces as shown in the diagram are important. The thickness of the letter equals the width; the diagram clearly shows the measurements. Each Y appears to be made up of five small cubes glued together. If, in fact, you were to make the Y's of small cubes you would need 125 of them. If you want to make the puzzle from cubes, start by making a pattern of the Y, so that all 25 pieces are the same. You can use alternately colored blocks for the Y piece, which will give the finished puzzle a checkerboard look.

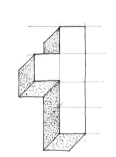

A different way to make the puzzle is to saw out the Y pieces with a band saw. Good sanding and some varnish will make the puzzle look professional.

The Cube des 25 Y was made by the French firm of Jeux Morize. This brain teaser with 236 solutions, has given people long hours of puzzle fun.

This diagram shows the proportions of the Y. You have to work very exactly, or the puzzle will not fit.

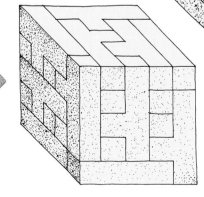

SOLUTION
One solution of the Y Cube is shown above.

THE DIABOLICAL CUBE

The French called this puzzle "diabolical" and it truly deserves the term. Six separate pieces together make a cube of 1¼ x 1¼ x 1¼ in. (3 x 3 x 3 cm). It really seems impossible to make a cube of so few pieces. Yet it is much easier to solve than the 25 Y Cube Puzzle. The puzzle was described in Hoffmann's book *Puzzles Old and New* from 1893. Hoffmann was a pseudonym for the British lawyer Angelo John Lewis (1839–1919). He was the first to write a comprehensive compilation of puzzles, and the book has since become the bible, so to speak, for puzzle collectors and puzzle enthusiasts.

The Diabolical Cube on this page was first described in the above book.

The diagram below shows the exact dimensions of the pieces of the puzzle. As an alternative, the pieces can be constructed from 27 loose cubes measuring 3⁄4 x 3⁄4 x 3⁄4 in. (18 x 18 x 18 mm). Lay them in the shape of the pieces and glue them together.

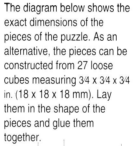

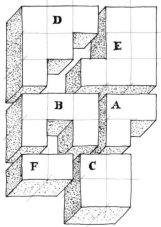

The French version of *The Diabolical Cube*, the Cube Diabolique, was manufactured between 1874 and 1908 by the Wattiliaux company of Paris.

HOW TO MAKE YOUR OWN DIABOLICAL CUBE

To begin with, you need a piece of 4 3⁄4 x 4 3⁄4 in. (12 x 12 cm) plywood of 3⁄4 in. (18 mm) thick. On this you copy the pieces as shown in the diagram. Be sure to work precisely, or the puzzle will not fit together properly afterwards. The dimensions of each piece are multiples of the 3⁄4 in. (18 mm) thickness of the plywood.

With a band saw or with a fine-toothed fret cut out the pieces. File the saw-edges and smooth them afterward with fine sandpaper. If you want to apply lacquer, be sure to file the pieces thinner. Otherwise, the thickness of the lacquer coat will prevent the pieces from fitting.

To store the puzzle, you can make a box with inside measurements of 4 3⁄8 x 4 3⁄8 x 4 3⁄8 in. (110 x 110 x 110 mm).

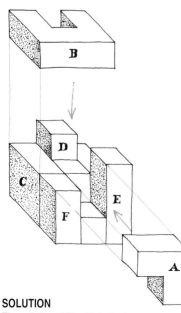

SOLUTION
The solution of The Diabolical Cube.

This Dutch *Diabolical Die Puzzle* was invented by Wil Strijbos from Holland, an ingenious puzzle inventor who has designed another absolute brain-teaser in the shape of this die puzzle.

A DIABOLICAL DIE

The Diabolical Die Puzzle, invented by Wil Strijbos from Holland, is a Dutch variation of a cube puzzle . The cube is built up using nine L-shaped pieces, each consisting of three dice. So all you need to make this puzzle are 27 dice and a tube of super glue! You can glue the pieces together in many ways to make more difficult puzzles. You can assemble the cube so that the same numbers appear on each side. Or you can design and make a cube puzzle where the outside faces of the cube have the same number of spots on a face and are arranged like a large die.

4	3
1	2

top

9	3
4	6
7	5

middle

	9
8	6
7	5

bottom

SOLUTION
The solution of the Diabolical Die. This solution is used for nine L-shaped pieces. A more difficult puzzle is to assemble the cube so that the same numbers appear on each side. Or you can, for example, design and make a cube puzzle where the outside faces of the cube have the same number of spots on a face and are arranged like a large die.

BILL'S SPLITTING HEADACHE

Bill Cutler has been intrigued by puzzles all his life. As a computer program designer and systems analyst he possesses skills he has often used to invent all sorts of tricky puzzles. He is particularly interested in inter-locking burr puzzles and puzzles involving the filling of boxes. He has often designed and used computer programs to find very difficult unique puzzles as well as to solve puzzles. And that while most people still have more problems with computers than with puzzles. Although, if you try Bill's Splitting Headache Puzzle, you may find that a computer program is easy by comparison!

At first sight Bill's puzzle looks similar to the one on the previous page created by Wil Strijbos. Forget it! If it's possible, this puzzle is even more difficult. There are several factors which add to its complexity. In the first place not all the pieces are identical. Secondly, in principle each piece is made up of three cubes, but some of them have been cut in half. Thirdly . . . yes there is another difficulty, but you have to try and find that one yourself. Good luck!

HOW TO MAKE BILL'S HEADACHE

What do you need? Just 27 wooden cubes, glue and a saw. Take 14 cubes in one color and 13 in another. What do you have to do? That is a lot harder. Study the diagram carefully to see how the pieces are made. It is vital that you make the pieces of your puzzle identical to those shown in the diagram, otherwise the puzzle will not fit properly together. A few of the cubes have been sawed in half. To do this you need a very thin saw-blade. The pieces which you saw in half should be one saw width wider in one dimension. Then when you saw them in half you get an exact half of a cube. Draw a line across the center of these cubes and saw them accurately in half. Make sure you use the same color for the cubes you cut as indicated in the diagram.Then glue the pieces together as shown. Of course it would be really great if, when you put the puzzle together, the grains of the sawed-through cubes would flow into one another. Then you would no longer be able to see which cubes have been halved and which haven't. Accuracy is vital when making this puzzle. The better it fits together, the harder it is to solve and the more professional it looks.

The Splitting Headache was designed by computer designer and systems analyst Bill Cutler. The puzzle was produced and put on the market in 1991 by J. M. McFarland of Chicago.

All nine pieces of the puzzle are shown in the diagram. Success depends on the accuracy used in reproducing these pieces.

SOLUTION
This diagram also shows the solution of this puzzle. Layer A is the bottom layer. On top of A goes B etc.
In layer B both pieces meet halfway to form a cube.

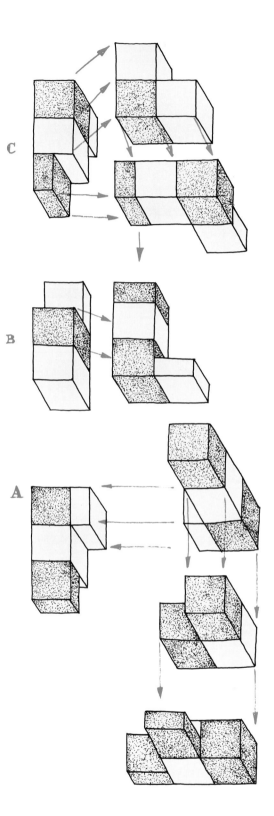

C

B

A

MATCHSTICK PUZZLES

Matchstick puzzles are often printed on the back of matchboxes. How often have you sat in a bar, restaurant or just at home racking your brains over such a simple looking puzzle involving a couple of matches? Do you think the inventor of this little object could have imagined what he was doing to us? In the course of time a wide range of uses for the match, apart from lighting, have been invented. Think of those people who spend whole winters building the Empire State Building from these little pieces of wood.

These pages contain a number of examples of matchstick puzzles, some of which date back to the beginning of this century. The two books of matchstick puzzle diagrams are fine examples of design of that era and are beautifully illustrated with colorful drawings.

Bryant and May published a sequel to *Fun Among the Matches.* This book was issued in 1911. Both works clearly illustrate the influence of Art Nouveau with its beautiful waving lines.

Use BRYANT & MAY'S SWAN VESTAS
THE SMOKER'S MATCH.

Arrange 10 matches to form a House instead of the two Wine Glasses.
6.

BUILDERS PUZZLE

Use BRYANT & MAY'S SAFET

STICKTRIC

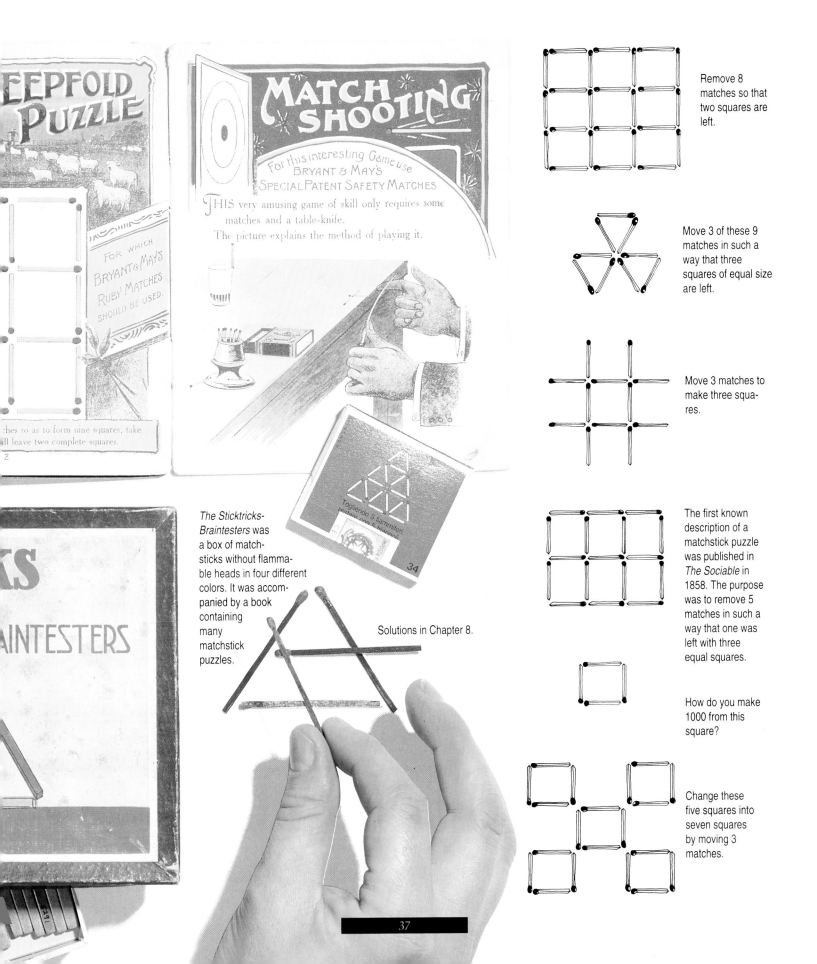

EEPFOLD PUZZLE

FOR WHICH BRYANT&MAYS RUBY MATCHES SHOULD BE USED.

...ches so as to form nine squares, take ...ll leave two complete squares.

2

MATCH SHOOTING

For this interesting Game use
BRYANT & MAYS
SPECIAL PATENT SAFETY MATCHES

THIS very amusing game of skill only requires some matches and a table-knife.
The picture explains the method of playing it.

Togliendo 5 fiammiferi...
34

The Sticktricks-Braintesters was a box of matchsticks without flammable heads in four different colors. It was accompanied by a book containing many matchstick puzzles.

Solutions in Chapter 8.

...KS
...AINTESTERS

Remove 8 matches so that two squares are left.

Move 3 of these 9 matches in such a way that three squares of equal size are left.

Move 3 matches to make three squares.

The first known description of a matchstick puzzle was published in *The Sociable* in 1858. The purpose was to remove 5 matches in such a way that one was left with three equal squares.

How do you make 1000 from this square?

Change these five squares into seven squares by moving 3 matches.

A DIFFICULT CASE?

It is often true that once you know the answer to a puzzle or problem, it seems easy. But until you know the answer... This is especially true for the Difficult Case. It is a purse with a padlock. The keys are in the purse. How do you get them out without breaking, tearing or cutting anything or forcing the lock?

In 1975 Michael Weber wanted to use a closed purse for a conjuring trick. One night he dreamed about a strange way of opening and closing a purse. In the morning he tried it out, and it worked! He showed the trick to a couple of famous conjurers, Dai Vernon and Charlie Miller, and neither had ever seen it.

Weber realized that he could also apply this to standard bank money sacks. He tried it out at a bank on Long Island. He asked the official to put something in a money sack and then seal it. She put her watch in the sack and locked it. Weber held the sack for less than a minute under the counter and then gave the girl the sack and her watch back separately. The sack was still closed.

Weber wrote to the directors of the bank and informed them that their money sacks could be opened invisibly and suggested a number of changes. The bank took his advice.

A few years later he gave a lecture at a conjurers' conference and afterward he was introduced to an employee of the IRS. This man had discovered that the sealed sacks belonging to the IRS could also be opened using Weber's method. Once again Weber designed the changes which were made to these sacks.

HOW TO MAKE AN IMPOSSIBLE PURSE

You only need a couple of things: a leather purse as illustrated, a padlock and a ring of ¼-⅜ in. (6-10 mm) diameter. Make a hole in the purse under the zipper on the side where the fastener sits when the zipper is closed. Thread the ring through this hole and squeeze it shut. And then: just put the keys in the purse, close the zipper and thread the padlock through the eye of the zipper and the ring. And now see who can get the keys out.

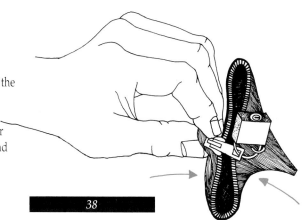

SOLUTION:
In order to open the purse you allow the teeth of the zipper to glide through the zipper case. You allow the sides of the zipper to bend outwards as shown in the diagram. The purse remains locked but the keys can be removed.

THE HIDDEN COIN

This *Trick Coin Box* was designed and made in 1981 by the British puzzle designer Mike Duffy. It looks so simple, but how does it open?

It looks impossible, but this book has already shown many puzzles that look impossible but are not! There is a coin in a box. You can see it through the slot in the lid. So it must be able to be removed, but how? It just takes a simple movement, namely to spin it around, to open the box. Unfortunately we have to give you the solution to this one, so you can make it to puzzle other people.

SOLUTION

Small metal rods which hold the lid in place are hidden in the lid. The rods slide out when the box is spun, thereby releasing the lid.

HOW TO MAKE THIS BOX

Materials you need:
1. A bar of wood, 5 7⁄8 x 5 7⁄8 in. (15 x 15 mm) thick and 11 in. (28 cm) long.
2. Two sheets of plywood, 2 3⁄4 x 2 3⁄4 in. (7 x 7 cm)
3. A block of wood, 13⁄8 x 13⁄8 in. (35 x 35 mm) large and 5⁄8 in. (15 mm) thick.
4. A wooden molding slat, 1 in. (24 mm) wide and 12 in. (30 cm) long (1⁄8 in. (3 mm) thick).
5. Four metal rods of 1⁄2 in. (1 cm) in length and 1⁄4 in. (6 mm) diameter.

As the diagram shows, saw the wooden piece (1) into four equal pieces measuring 2 3⁄4 in. (7 cm) long with an angle of 45° at the ends. Glue these together onto the sheet of plywood. This is the lid. You then glue the block of wood (3) exactly in the middle of the other sheet of plywood. This is the box. Then place the lid on the box and drill 5⁄16 in. (7 mm) holes on four sides of the lid to 3⁄16 in. (5 mm) deep in the box. Consult the diagram on how to do this. Now you glue the piece of molding slat to the sides of the lid to cover the holes. Next you have to make a slot in the box for the coin to fit through. Use a 1⁄8 in. (3 mm) drill bit to drill a row of holes next to one another. Cut away the wood in between the holes with a small chisel or knife to create a slot. Do the same in the lid. This slot must be small enough to prevent the coin from coming out of the box. You should then round off the ends of the metal rods and push them into the holes in the lid from the inside. Put the coin in place and let the lid fall carefully over the box. A quick shake and you're ready to puzzle your friends.

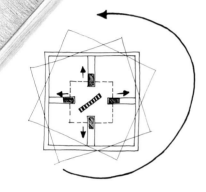

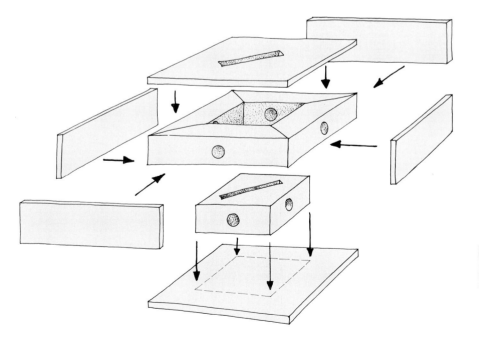

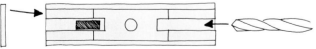

The diagram shows how it is assembled.

THE SECRET BOX

If you have ever been to a magic show, you may have seen a famous magic trick with a large box with chains and padlocks. Even with the chest locked the magician got out. And you never knew how he does it!

There are many magic boxes and crates of this type in the world of puzzles. They have been made for many years now in various countries. In England, boxes were made which looked like a pile of books or just one book. The opening was hidden behind a secret slide. Professor Hoffmann's book describes such a puzzle; The Psycho Matchbox Puzzle which looks at first sight like an ordinary box with a lid. But what appears to be the lid is false, and the real lid looks like part of the box. If you hold the box upside down a pin slides across thereby releasing the real lid.

Another fine example of these boxes comes from Italy. Book type puzzle boxes were made in Sorrento and Naples around 1920–1930. The lid looks as though it has been shaped like a loose book on top of the pile of books. Wrong. First you have to find the secret compartment in which the key is kept, then you have to detect the slide which masks the keyhole. A two-step puzzle box.

It won't surprise anyone to learn that there are also many Japanese versions of this puzzle. Japanese boxes with secret locks were exported to the West even before 1920. One side has sliding panels which enable the side to be moved a small distance. This makes it possible to shift another side a little, and after several such moves finally the lid can be opened. One example exists, dating from 1960, which requires 66 moves to open the box! These boxes are often beautifully decorated with veneer made of various types of wood. This wood mosaic is called "Yoseki." The intricate patterns often disguise the sliding panels which open the box.

This *Secret Box* was designed in 1986 by Robert Jackson from Riverside, California. Jackson designed the box for magicians, for use in their magic acts.

HOW TO MAKE A SECRET BOX

The example which we show here is only one of many kinds. It looks very complicated, but the solution is very simple. The principle behind this little box is that the corner pieces camouflage the secret fastener.

This box measures 2 3⁄4 x 1 3⁄4 x 3 3⁄4 in. (7 x 4.5 x 9.5 cm), but you can make it as big as you like. The base is made of a piece of plywood measuring 2 3⁄4 x 31⁄2 in. (7 x 9 cm). You glue the front and back, each 15⁄8 x 21⁄2 in. (4 x 6.5 cm), and one side measuring 15⁄8 x 33⁄8 in. (4 x 8.5 cm) onto this base. In this example the plywood is 1⁄10 in. (2.5 mm) thick. The sliding lid slides between two slats which have been fixed to the sides of the box. On one side this slat has indeed been mounted onto the side panel, but on the other side it is in fact only supported by the corners of the front and back pieces of the box. When the box is finished, it looks as though the slats are firmly fastened on both sides, which is what it is meant to look like. Since they are not fastened to the side of the box, the side can rotate about the pin shown, thereby opening the box. The side should fit tightly so a good push on the side is needed to open it. Two slats of 3⁄4 x 15⁄8 in. (2 x 4 cm) are mounted onto each corner. Look at the diagram to see how to do this but be careful: on only three of the four corners these slats are not only glued to the box but also to each other. On the fourth corner, the right hand side of the loose panel (from the viewer's vantage point), one slat is only glued to the secret lid (the loose side panel) and is not attached to the slat round the corner on the front.

Next, two more vertical slats are glued onto the two side pieces which are a bit narrower than those on the corners. On the fixed side this is only decoration, but on the loose panel one of these slats is the hinging point. The panel turns on two nails. The other nails are for decoration. Two screw-eyes are then screwed onto the front and the lid. Hang the padlock on these, put the keys in the box and who's going to find the solution?

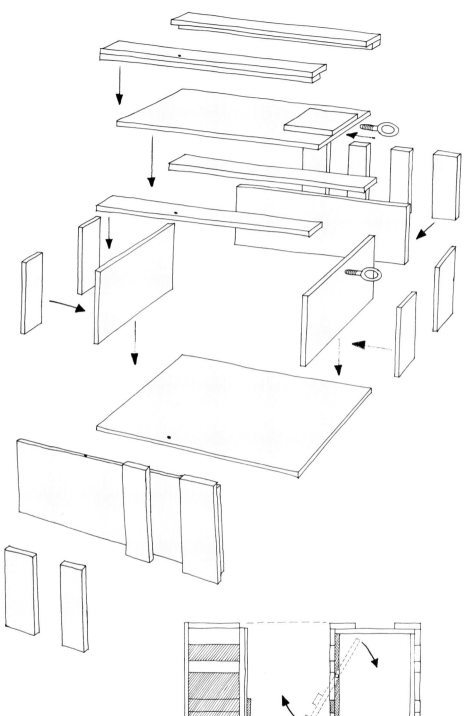

SOLUTION

To make the box we have to show you the solution. The diagram shows you how to open the box in a very simple way.

It is difficult to explain how to make this puzzle. The best thing to do is to study the diagram carefully. This shows clearly how the puzzle is constructed.

TWO ELEPHANTS WITH A SECRET

These two beautiful bookends come from Sri Lanka. They are made of ebony inlaid with ivory. However, these elephants watch over more than just the books which you place between them.
Each wooden book contains a secret compartment which can only be opened by knowing the "trick." By sliding the spine of the book downward a second slide appears which is the lid to the hidden compartment. It is an ideal space for hiding small things such as love letters, money and jewelry, although maybe the last two would be safer in a bank!

Secret compartments have been built into boxes, cabinets and furniture for centuries. I'm sure everyone knows of a grandfather's desk or a piece of furniture or a box with its secret compartment. I know of a little desk on which two books stand, finely bound in leather. However, if you take them out you find out that they are two wooden boxes with secret compartments. Very ingenious!
The oldest secret compartment box in Jerry Slocum's collection dates back to about 1800.

These *Secret Elephant Bookends* were made in Sri Lanka. They are based on the same principle as the secret boxes described elsewhere in this book. The inventor and maker of these bookends has long been forgotten. But it is clear that whoever made them must have been a great craftsman.

HOW TO MAKE THESE BOOKENDS

Unfortunately we don't have the space here to describe this fantastic example of craftsmanship step-by-step. You would have to be a very experienced wood carver and cabinetmaker to be able to make this yourself. The books have been carved out of one piece of wood. The success of such puzzles greatly depends on the accuracy with which they are made. If the joints don't all fit together exactly then you can immediately see how to open it!
If you want to try to make it, the diagram shows how the books are constructed. A dovetail joint enables the spine of the book to slide downward thereby revealing the slide for the hidden compartment. When the bookends are assembled and in place, nobody can see that they contain a secret space!
The books are mirror images of each other. Instead of elephants you can use other figures, like horses, dogs etc.

If you study the drawing carefully you may be able to make the puzzle– that is if you are highly skilled in wood carving!

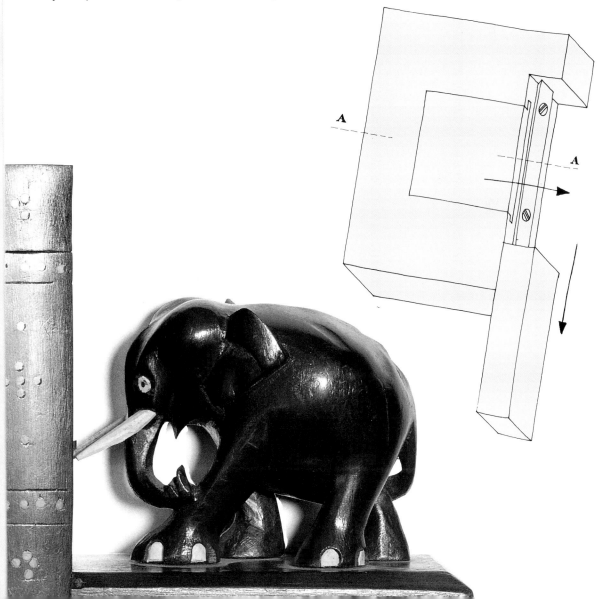

PAPER MAGIC

Paper and cardboard have always been popular materials for making puzzles. They can be cheap of course, but at the same time beautiful and provide challenging puzzles. At the end of the last century the advertising world especially in the U.S., made widespread use of these materials, when hundreds of companies advertised their products using cardboard puzzles. The puzzle was richly covered with charming illustrations and slogans advertising the claims of superiority of the product. This page shows four puzzles of this type. Three of these, the Farnsworth Puzzle, the Yates Puzzle and the Skipper Sardines Puzzle, all work along the same lines. The Nye Puzzle is a different type. Not only is it great fun to solve the puzzles, but it is also very amusing to see how products were advertised in 1884.

MAKE YOUR OWN VERSION OF A PAPER PUZZLE

The Farnsworth, Yates and Skipper puzzles are made as follows:

You need a thick piece of paper measuring 4 x 8 in. (10 x 20 cm). Fold the width in half. The diagram shows the pieces you have to cut out of the paper. Cut out the map, the boot and the ring and assemble them.

Exactly, but how do you solve it? To find out, study the diagram carefully. Slide oblong C over the thin leg of oblong piece A. Then push the boot B, folded open, through that leg of oblong piece A. Finally, slide the small oblong A over the end of the folded boot. Open out card A and your puzzle should look exactly like the last diagram!

SOLUTION

The solutions to the Farnsworth, Yates and Skipper puzzle are very simple for the maker, but the person who has to do the puzzles will be faced with a lot more problems. To solve each puzzle you just follow the instruction diagrams in reverse order and take it apart again step-by-step.

The baker in the barrel was a bread and biscuit advertisement for the Nye Company of New York. This *Best Bread Puzzle* is yet another version of the cardboard puzzle like, for example, the *Yates Puzzle.*

The Skipper Sardines Puzzle was circulated as advertisement by Angus Watson & Co. A can of sardines is suspended from the picture of the skipper. The trick is to separate the two from one another.

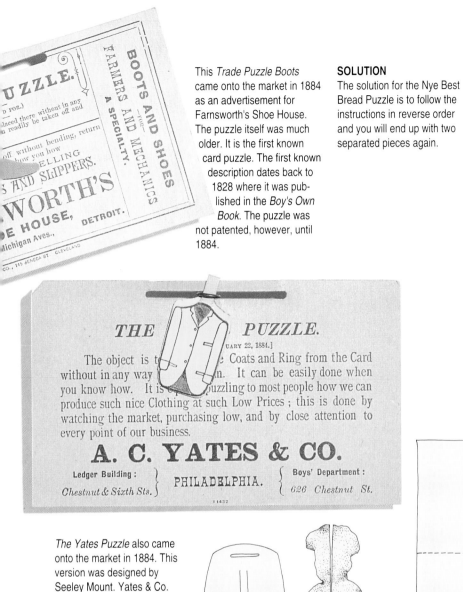

This *Trade Puzzle Boots* came onto the market in 1884 as an advertisement for Farnsworth's Shoe House. The puzzle itself was much older. It is the first known card puzzle. The first known description dates back to 1828 where it was published in the *Boy's Own Book*. The puzzle was not patented, however, until 1884.

SOLUTION

The solution for the Nye Best Bread Puzzle is to follow the instructions in reverse order and you will end up with two separated pieces again.

HOW TO MAKE THE NYE BEST BREAD PUZZLE

Take a sheet of transparent paper and trace the drawing in the photo. The puzzle consists of two parts: a barrel and a head with a long tab on it. Transfer the drawing onto thick paper or thin cardboard.

Cut out the barrel and make two long slots lengthwise and a small slot at the top. The diagram shows where to make these cuts.

Then cut out the head with the tab and cut through this lengthwise to 3⁄16 in. (5 mm) from the base. There, just like on the diagram, you make a hole which is 1⁄32 in. (1 mm) wider than the middle strip in the barrel. Make sure you don't tear the bottom of the tab!

How do you assemble the puzzle? Push the middle strip of the barrel through the slot above it. Through this loop you push half of the head and pull it straight so that the strip is in the hole at the base of the tab. You then push back the loop and the head is stuck to the barrel.

The Yates Puzzle also came onto the market in 1884. This version was designed by Seeley Mount. Yates & Co. was a clothing firm, so instead of Farnsworth's boot, this puzzle depicted a jacket.

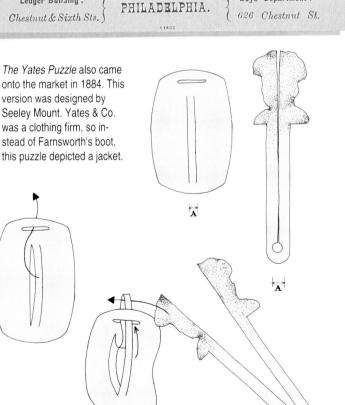

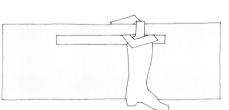

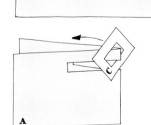

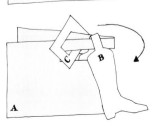

If you follow the directions shown on the diagrams, you should be able to make these puzzles without any problem.

THE PICK-A-PEG PUZZLE

Just take the puzzle apart. After all, it doesn't look too difficult. If you try this puzzle, you'll find that it is much harder than it looks. This puzzle is known as the Pick-a-Peg. It was invented by J. D. Boyle and patented on May 10, 1949. That is also the year it was put on the market in America.

The seemingly simple little puzzle consists of two round pegs which pass through holes and cross in an octagonal piece of wood. If you try the puzzle you will soon realize that pulling, tugging and pushing the pieces won't help in solving it. It is impossible! How can the thickened ends of the pegs cross one another? Only the go-getter, the dedicated puzzle addict may be able to discover the solution. Unless of course you read the solution first!

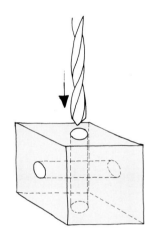

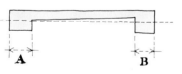

When making this puzzle it is wise to study the diagram carefully and make the cuts and holes very accurately or else you will neither be able to assemble nor disassemble it.

J. D. Boyle's Pick-a-Peg Puzzle dating from 1949 has already driven many people to despair. For many, this sophisticated puzzle is insolvable.

HOW TO MAKE THIS PUZZLE

You need two round pegs with a diameter of 5⁄16 in. (8 mm) and a length of 2 in. (5 cm), and a piece of wood measuring 1¼ x 1¼ in., ¾ in. (3 x 3 cm, 2 cm) thick. Use a 3⁄8 in. (9 mm) drill bit to drill two holes in the central piece which cross each other exactly in the middle. In one of the drill holes drill another hole sloping toward the flat side of the central shape. The diagram shows how this hole must be angled. Make sure that the hole is not visible from the outside of the wood.

You then use this piece of wood to make an octagon by sawing off the corners with a fine tenon saw.

Now make the two pegs: Saw out the middle part of both pegs over the whole length (see diagram). The ends are ¼ in. (7 mm) long; that means you saw off 2 – ½= 1½ in. (50 – 14 = 36 mm).

Note: as the diagram shows, you saw out that piece with a shallow angle. You begin at the center of the diameter of the peg and saw until the peg is only 1⁄16 in. (2 mm) thick. Next, using a fine file, smooth the edges. Also note that one of the ends is 1⁄32 in. (1 mm) shorter (A,B). Sand everything nice and smooth with fine sandpaper and you are ready to try out the puzzle.

AN EXTRA TRICK

Put the assembled puzzle in water for a few hours so that it becomes soaked through. The wood will then swell up making the puzzle impossible to solve. Then allow the puzzle to dry for a few hours so that it looks dry from the outside.

Now invite your victim to solve the puzzle. However clever the puzzle fan is, he won't manage to unravel this one! The wood is still swollen. It will take several days before the wood has shrunk back to normal size and the puzzle can once again be solved.

SOLUTION

The secret of the solution to the puzzle is based on the tapering of the sawed-out portion of the pegs and the fact that the end of one peg is a little bit shorter.

How to go about it:

1. Pull the shortest end into the hole in the octagonal piece.
2. Pull the other peg with the thinnest side into the hole in the octagonal piece.
3. Rotate the second peg slowly to the left and you will feel the end cross over the other peg and come free.

THE CROSS PUZZLE

The puzzle appears to consist of two identical pieces of wood which can easily be taken apart. But of course it is never that simple. The two parts are solidly joined together and there is only one way of taking them apart and now we will tell you how to solve it.

The Japanese puzzle expert and collector Nob Yoshigahara has a collection of 2000 puzzles and 10,000 puzzle books, and he has published over 30 books of his own on this subject. He is the inventor of this cross puzzle. The puzzle is based on a puzzle dating from 1910, the Johnny Walker Trick Matchbox. In order to open this matchbox you had to spin it fast on a table so that a number of pins in the box shot out due to centrifugal force. The idea was patented by Herbert Taylor in England in 1910.

And 70 years later Yoshigahara invented a new variation which was first marketed in 1981.

This *Dualock* was designed by Nob Yoshigahara and put on the market in 1981 by Puzzland Hikimi in Japan. However, the idea for such a puzzle dates back to 1910, when the Johnny Walker Trick Matchbox was invented. The basic principles under-lying both puzzles is that cen-trifugal force causes a number of pins to shoot out, thereby enabling the puzzle to be opened.

SOLUTION

This puzzle therefore belongs to the spin-to-open category. But Yoshigahara has added an extra difficulty. You have to lay the puzzle on a table. You then spin it around, turn it over and spin it again. Only then will the puzzle open. This is because small ball bearings are hidden in the wooden bars which secure the locking pins in a certain position. The construction diagram clearly shows how this puzzle is made.

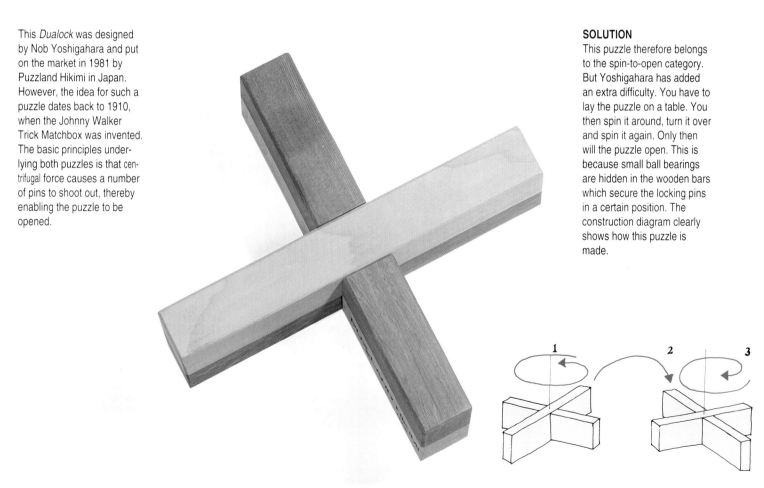

HOW TO MAKE A CROSS PUZZLE

What you need:
1. Two small wooden bars of 3⁄4 x 3⁄4 in. (20 x 20 mm) thick and 51⁄2 in. (14 cm) long;
2. Four small wooden bars of 3⁄4 x 3⁄4 in. (20 x 20 mm) thick and 2 3⁄8 in. (6 cm) long;
3. Four round wooden rods with a diameter of 5⁄16 in. (8 mm) and 15⁄8 in. (4 cm) long;
4. Four ball bearings with a diameter of 5⁄16 in (8 mm).

You drill a hole with a diameter of 1⁄2 in. (12 mm) exactly in the center of the two 51⁄2 in. (14 cm) long bars. At both ends of the bars drill a hole with a diameter of 3⁄8 in. (10 mm) and 5⁄8 in. (15 mm) deep. Consult the diagram very carefully because the center hole is on a different side of the bar than the holes at the ends.

In the four short bars drill a hole 3⁄8 in. (10 mm) wide and 2 in. (5 cm) deep lengthwise in the bar. You then drill another hole 3⁄8 in. (10 mm) wide and 5⁄8 in. (15 mm) deep in the sides of the bars. Make sure that all these holes are at exactly the same distance from the end as the holes in the long bars. They have to fit together properly. Now it is time to assemble the parts of the cross. You can see from the diagram that two short bars are glued onto a long one. However, before you glue them together, you have to place one steel ball bearing and a wooden rod in each end. The diagram shows how to do this. When the glue has dried, sand it all until smooth.
In order to assemble the two legs into a cross, you push the rods right inside and carefully twist one leg around and set it in the slot of the other leg. Give it a slight shake and the puzzle is ready.
If you find that the legs don't fit together, then file away the space between the two glued bars until they do fit with about 1⁄64 in. (half a mm) to spare.

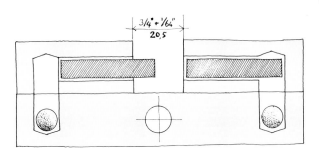

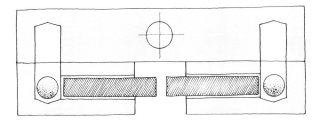

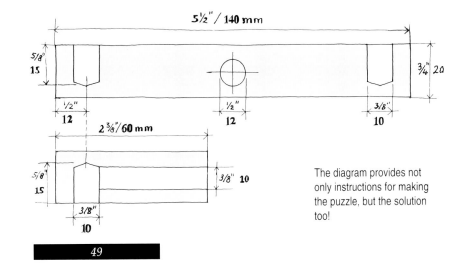

The transparent version shows how the system works when the puzzle is closed. When this version is spun, you see how the pins slide out.

The diagram provides not only instructions for making the puzzle, but the solution too!

KUMIKI PUZZLES

3.

Interlocking solid puzzles.
Objective: Disassembly and
assembly to solve the puzzle.

Pages 50–67

Japan is subject to earthquakes almost daily. Some are barely noticeable but a brick building would be affected by them sooner or later. This is one of the reasons why for centuries now, buildings in Japan have been constructed according to a special technique. Many buildings are made entirely of wood. These are constructed in such a way that no nails are used. The house is fitted together like a puzzle, whereby the structure remains much more flexible. Nails and other metal components would bend, but these wooden structures can withstand any type of tremor and just settle back into place again afterwards.

At the end of the nineteenth century Tsunetaro Yamanaka (1874–1954) from the Hakone district applied this technique, which was also used for interlocking puzzles (see elsewhere in this book), to make figurative puzzles for the first time. He constructed interlocking models of houses, pagodas and gates which fit together without the use of nails or glue. He later extended his range of subjects to include boats, airplanes and cars. The puzzles were called Kumiki Puzzles. Yamanaka's sons carried on the tradition and produced new shapes based on architecture and the animal world. Today, Kumiki Puzzles are still being made in Hakone. The industry there has grown to six companies with a turnover of 500,000 dollars per year, and this complicated Japanese construction method has become known all over the world. The ancient Japanese architects must have been some sort of super puzzle makers!

Kumiki puzzles are mostly made of Cheek wood, but cherry wood and Zelkova wood are also suitable. There are four different Kumiki techniques: oshi, mawashi, kendon and sayubiki. The first means push: these puzzles have a key piece which has to be pushed out. Puzzles based on the mawashi principle have a piece which has to be twisted in order to solve the puzzle. In kendon puzzles you have to remove a piece by moving it up and down or from left to right. With sayubiki, two key pieces have to be removed simultaneously.

This *Kumiki of a Monoplane* is a later version of the planes from 1930. This was also designed by Tsunetaro Yamanaka in 1937 and manufactured by his own firm.

This plane with pilot was made by Tsunetaro Yamanaka and dates from about 1930. It is a fairly simple Kumiki.

HOW TO MAKE A KUMIKI PLANE

These figures are best made of wood with a short fiber, such as beech.

The advantage of Kumiki Puzzles is that they can be made whatever size you prefer. Therefore it is not necessary to provide all the detailed dimensions for you to make your own puzzle. The important thing is to make sure the slots are in the right places so that the pieces fit together.

The plane has been photographed completed and disassembled, so that you can see all the parts clearly. In addition we have made a diagram of the two parts of the fuselage as these contain all the slots for the wings etc. Copy these parts accurately and use your imagination when making the wings and tail.

The assembly should be no problem so we leave that to you too. Good luck.

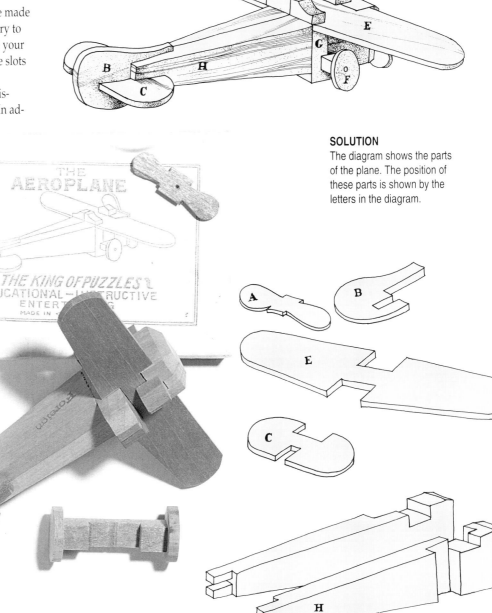

SOLUTION
The diagram shows the parts of the plane. The position of these parts is shown by the letters in the diagram.

This disassembled Kumiki by Tsunetaro Yamanaka also represents a plane. This version was produced by S. T. (The King of Puzzles) from Japan.

The drawing shows the two parts of the fuselage with clear indications where the slots for the wing and tail have to be made. Provided you follow the instructions for the slots, you can design the plane according to your own taste.

PUZZLE KNOTS

A burr interlocking puzzle consists of a number of pieces which fit into each other in an ingenious manner. It often looks impossible to take them apart and even more impossible to fit them together again! For some interlocking puzzles one piece provides the key to the puzzle, hence the name key piece. This piece has to be removed before the puzzle can be taken apart. When the puzzle is being assembled, this is the last piece which holds the puzzle together.

The history of these puzzles is rather vague. However, we do know that they were already being made in the eighteenth century in both Asia and Europe. The toy manufacturer Bestelmeier included two examples of interlocking puzzles in his *Toy Catalog* in 1803: the big and the small Devil's Hoof. The big one consisted of no fewer than 24 parts. The small one was a six piece burr.

Hoffmann also included two of this type of puzzle in his *Puzzles Old and New*, published in 1893.

During the course of the nineteenth century six part interlocking puzzles became increasingly more compact. Puzzles were developed which consisted of balls and cubes which at first sight looked impossible to separate!

Since the 1930s the Japanese manufacturers have mainly determined and dominated the market with many figurative versions as well as the traditional interlocking puzzles (see pages on Kumikis).

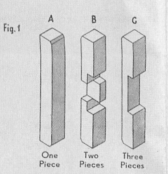

These *Spears Puzzle Knots* were manufactured in Bavaria around 1910, but packaged and marketed in England. Such six-piece knots first appeared in *Bestelmeier's Toy Catalog* in 1803.

HOW TO MAKE THESE PUZZLE KNOTS

The first knot is made of six bars, 1⁄2 x 1⁄2 in. (12 x 12 mm) thick and 2 3⁄4 in. (7 cm) long. Five of these bars have notches and are divided into a group of two identical bars and a group of three (see diagram). The measurements of the notches are indicated by the letter A
(A=1⁄2 in. (12 mm), is the thickness of the bars).
Using a small fretsaw, saw the notches out of the bars. Use a 1⁄4 in. (6 mm) thick square file to file all the notches nice and smooth. Sand the pieces smooth. Now try to assemble the puzzle to see if any parts stick. If they do file the notches some more. Finally, you can paint or stain the puzzle.

The second knot is made of strips of wood 3⁄4 x 5⁄16 in. (20 x 8 mm) thick and 2 3⁄8 in. (6 cm) long. The diagram shows the proportions of the various pieces. Five pieces look identical, but one of them is different: the notch is shorter. The notch is 1 1⁄4 in. (31 mm) long and 1⁄8 in. (3 mm) deep on four of the pieces. The notch on the fifth piece is 1⁄8 in. (3 mm) shorter. Be careful because that piece only goes from one side, so one end is 1⁄8 in. (3 mm) longer than the other end. The last piece has an extra notch measuring 1⁄8 x 3⁄4 in. (3 x 20 mm) on one side of the center. As with the first knot, file everything smooth and assemble the puzzle to check that it fits. Then paint it according to your own taste.

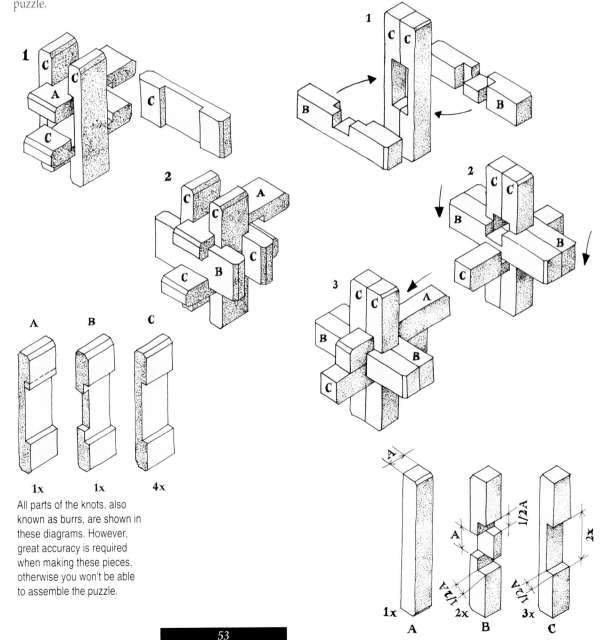

All parts of the knots, also known as burrs, are shown in these diagrams. However, great accuracy is required when making these pieces, otherwise you won't be able to assemble the puzzle.

THE CAGE

This intricate puzzle belongs to the interlocking puzzle category previously discussed. The puzzle on which this cage is based appears on page 52. There is no end to the variations on this burr or knot– and ever more and difficult puzzles are being developed. The cage consists of eight solid burrs, which means that nowhere inside the burrs are there any empty spaces. In this version the burrs are different at every corner which makes the puzzle very complicated and extremely difficult to solve. The puzzle in the photo, having eight different burrs at the corners, would take too many pages to describe comprehensibly, so here we will just describe a simpler version with the same burr at the eight corners.

HOW TO MAKE A CAGE PUZZLE

In this version, the knot on page 52 is repeated 8 times. The diagram shows the different pieces.
The measurements of the pieces are 3⁄4 x 3⁄4 in. (20 x 20 mm), 6 1⁄4 in. (16 cm) long. The measurement of A is 3⁄4 in. (20 mm). You need four of the key piece (two, without notches). You need twelve of the piece with notches on one side (3), and eight of the double notched piece (2). The notches should always be sawed out from either side of the center of each piece with a fretsaw. File and sand the sawn surfaces and edges smooth to make the pieces fit properly. To make the puzzle look nice you can either oil or stain it. Paint will reduce the size of the notches and increase the thickness of the pieces so that the puzzle is likely not to fit properly if painted.

The Burr Cage is an elaborate interlocking puzzle. The designer and maker of the model shown is Gary Foshee of Seattle. The puzzle was made in 1980. A similar cage burr was shown in Bestelmeiers' Toy Catalog of 1803.

SOLUTION

To solve this puzzle you should use the solution to the Six Piece Burr on page 52. Follow the same order of assembly.

Observe in the diagram how the numbered pieces are positioned. Start with the four upright pieces marked 3. Then the two bottom pieces marked 3 in the bottom layer. Then the four pieces marked 1 in the bottom layer. Then the two top pieces in the bottom layer.

Repeat the above for the top layer.

Finally you put in the four key pieces.

The model made by Gary Foshee is much more complicated than the one shown in the diagram.

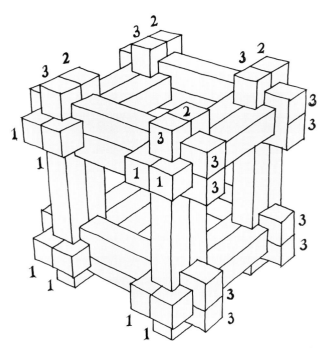

This diagram gives the exact size and shape of the different pieces of the cage burr.

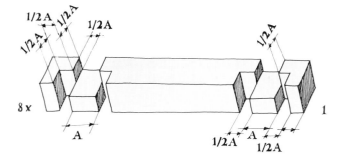

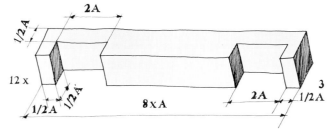

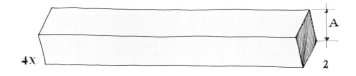

A WOODEN THREE-PIECE BURR

This three-piece interlocking puzzle is solved according to a principle that the Japanese call mawashi. It means that one piece must be turned in order to put the puzzle together or to take it apart. It creates a strong as well as an ingenious piece of woodwork. In his 1928 book *Puzzles in Wood* Wyatt recommended woodwork instructors to include this puzzle in their lessons as an example of good old-fashioned crafts-manship. To enhance its instructive value, each of the pieces could be made of a different type of wood. Another cage puzzle variation of this burr is the Boule Enfermée.

This *Three-Piece Burr* is an interlocking puzzle with the solution in a rotating key piece. It was described in Wyatt's *Puzzles in Wood* published in 1928 as being a good exercise for future car-penters and cabinetmakers.

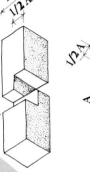

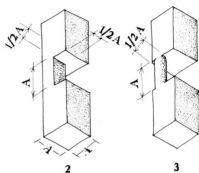

The illustration shows the interior of the puzzle: brilliant in its simplicity.

HOW TO MAKE THE THREE-PIECE BURR PUZZLE

For this puzzle you need three 1 7/16 x 1 7/16 in. (36 x 36 mm) pieces of wood with a length of 5 7/16 in. (13.8 cm) each. To determine the positions of the notches you measure from the center of each piece. Mark them with a pencil, using a 90° miter square to get the lines straight. Study the diagram closely for the dimensions of the notches. Use a backsaw to saw the notches. Then chip away the wood with a sharp chisel. Sand all the edges to size and smooth them. The center section of one piece is

filed and sanded round. The more accurately the pieces have been made the more difficult the puzzle will be. If you want to varnish the pieces remember that this will make the notches smaller and the pieces thicker. You can stain them and avoid this problem.

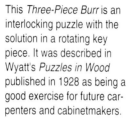

SOLUTION TO THE THREE-PIECE BURR
Piece 3 is put in piece 1.
Piece 2 can be put in position.
To fasten the puzzle turn piece 3 in position.

THE BOULE ENFERMÉE

This cage variation of the Three-Piece Burr Puzzle encages a wooden ball. Taking the puzzle apart is the only way to release it. The solution to this puzzle also lies in rotating the key pieces, in this case four. The diagram clearly shows the dimensions, number and proportions of the pieces. You can make the puzzle by using the diagram.

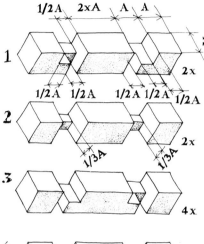

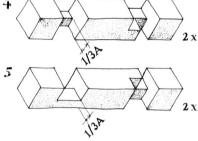

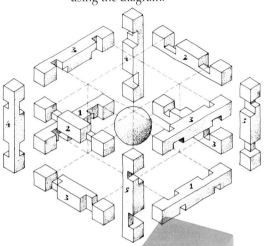

SOLUTION TO THE BOULE ENFERMÉE
Again, the mawashi principle is the key to this puzzle. But from here on the puzzle makers are on their own to find the position of all the pieces. Just follow the approach shown for the Three-Piece Burr.

The diagram shows all the parts of the Boule Enfermée. The dimensions and proportions should be followed with great precision when making the puzzle, to insure it will fit afterward.

The Boule Enfermée is an extension of the Three-Piece Burr. It was sold by the French manufacturer Arjeu in 1985.

VERNON WOOD PUZZLE

This interlocking puzzle by Vernon Wood is his personal variation on the Three-Piece Burr Puzzle. In Wyatt's 1928 book *Puzzles in Wood*, the Nine-Piece Burr Puzzle was described. This puzzle clearly illustrates that, on the basis of an existing puzzle, you can very well design and make your own variation and thereby create an entirely new puzzle. While experimenting should you really invent an original and difficult puzzle, don't forget to copyright or patent your design! In 1957 Vernon Wood made this puzzle and dedicated it to Jerry Slocum.

This *Nine-Piece Burr* was designed by Vernon Wood. It's a variation on the Three-Piece Burr. In 1928 Wyatts' book *Puzzles in Wood*, described a similar nine-piece burr. This specimen dates from 1957 and was dedicated to Jerry Slocum.

HOW TO MAKE THIS PUZZLE

The puzzle consists of six large pieces assembled around three smaller pieces. They are shown in the diagram. Five of the large pieces are identical. They are made of Meranti wood and measure 1⅜ x 3 ⅜ x ⅝ in. (35 x 86 x 16 mm). The sixth piece has a round middle section which enables it to turn and serve as the key piece.

Make the cuts by using a backsaw and chisel away the wood to make the notches. Then smooth the notches with a flat file, which you also use to smooth the round middle section.

The central assembly consists of three similar pieces. One, however, has a 5⁄16 x 5⁄16 in. (8 x 8 mm) cube glued in the middle notch. (Of course you can also make the notch half as deep while sawing it). File these pieces as you did the former. You can oil the pieces to protect them from greasy finger marks.

The diagram clearly shows the dimensions of the nine large and small pieces.

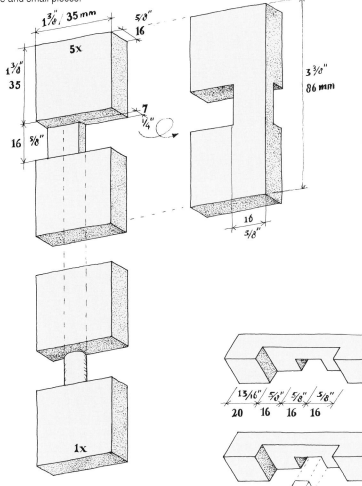

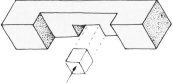

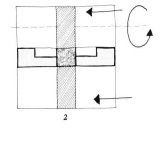

SOLUTION

Assemble the central cross as shown in the diagram. The diagrams give a view from one side.

Then take two large pieces. One of these is the key piece with the rounded middle section. Lay these flat on either side above and below the central cross (see diagram 1). The key piece is on top. Then you stand two pieces from right to left (diagram 2). Then you turn the key piece into a horizontal position and insert the remaining two pieces in the spaces under the key piece. Turn the key piece back and the puzzle fits together.

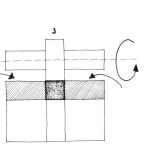

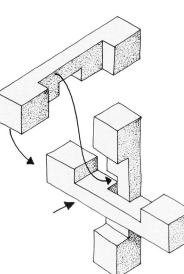

The puzzle actually consists of two parts. The central cross, constructed of three pieces of wood and the six wings of which one is the key piece which rotates to take the puzzle apart.

THE BILL CUTLER BIN CROSS

Earlier in this book you may have come across the Splitting Headache, a puzzle by Bill Cutler. It is an extremely difficult puzzle. A computer program designer and systems analyst, Bill Cutler is used to solving difficult problems, problems that many people could never solve. Not only is it his job, it is his hobby as well. With the computer he solves puzzles and invents new ones. If you thought that the Splitting Headache was difficult, get ready for this one. Bill's Drinking Glass Puzzle at first looks totally unsolvable. But don't despair. What goes into the glass must come out, or doesn't it?

The puzzle was manufactured and sold in 1991 by the Japanese Toyo Glass Co. Bill Cutler calls it his Bin Cross Puzzle.

Bill Cutler designed his *Bin Cross* on the computer and there is only one single solution to the puzzle. Bin Cross was put on the market in 1991 by the Japanese Toyo Glass Co.

HOW TO MAKE THE BIN CROSS PUZZLE

To keep it simple, we have replaced the glass with a cardboard cylinder with a bottom. If you have equipment for cutting glass or perhaps a lucite plastic cylinder, by all means use them. But this cardboard cylinder, though less attractive, is a simpler substitute to work with.

The puzzle consists of six 5⁄8 x 5⁄8 in. (14 x 14 mm) pieces of wood 4 1⁄4 in. (108 mm) long. They are notched as shown in the diagram. Saw the pieces with a fret saw and smooth all the surfaces with a 1⁄4 in. (6 to 7 mm) wide square file. For easier assembly the notches can be filed slightly wider. The pieces must be able to slide easily in relation to one another. Therefore they should be sanded really smooth. The cardboard "glass" should be made of a 4 in. (10 cm) long cylinder, 2 3⁄8 in. (6 cm) diameter. Cut four recgtangular holes of 1 1⁄4 x 5⁄8 in. (30 x 16 mm). One set of holes is vertical, the other horizontal. Consult the diagram for their exact positions. Attach a cardboard disk or a plastic lid to the cylinder to form the bottom.

SOLUTION

The diagram with instructions for making the puzzle gives part of the solution at the same time. It shows three sets of pieces of wood. The arrows and the letters at each end give the direction in which they are to be put in the cylinder. The small diagram indicates the slot in the cylinder.

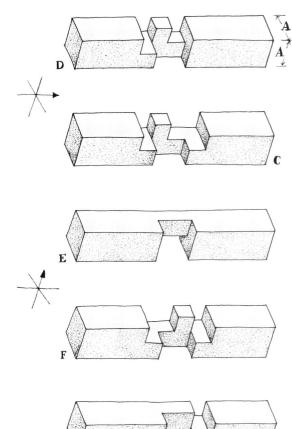

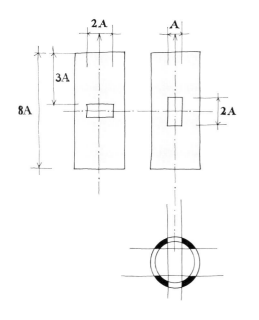

The diagram shows both the dimensions of the different pieces and directions for the solution.

THE FINNISH DIAGONAL BURR

Interlocking puzzles are a worldwide phenomenon. Finland too has a tradition of making this kind of puzzle. The remarkable feature of the Finnish puzzles is that the pieces of wood are oriented diagonally. This makes a very unusual looking puzzle.

These diagonal interlocking puzzles have even found their way to the National Museum in Helsinki. One of them is from Kontiolahti and dates from around 1910. A diagonal burr was patented by Chandler in 1888. Thirteen pieces make up this puzzle. An even older diagonal burr was advertised in *The Youth Companion* in 1875.

This diagonal puzzle is known throughout Finland. Matti Linkola was told by some old lumberjacks that the puzzle had been around in the logging camps for over 50 years.

The photo shows two variations of the original 13-piece puzzle. One consists of 15 pieces and we will give a description of how to make it and provide the solution to this one. The other one has no fewer than 74 pieces. This puzzle was made by Matti Linkola. However, you are advised not to start on this one until you are very adept at the 15-piece one, because once taken apart you may never get it together again.

This 74-part interlocking puzzle will test your patience to its limits and putting it together requires nerves of steel. It has been produced since 1985 by the Finnish puzzle expert Matti Linkola.

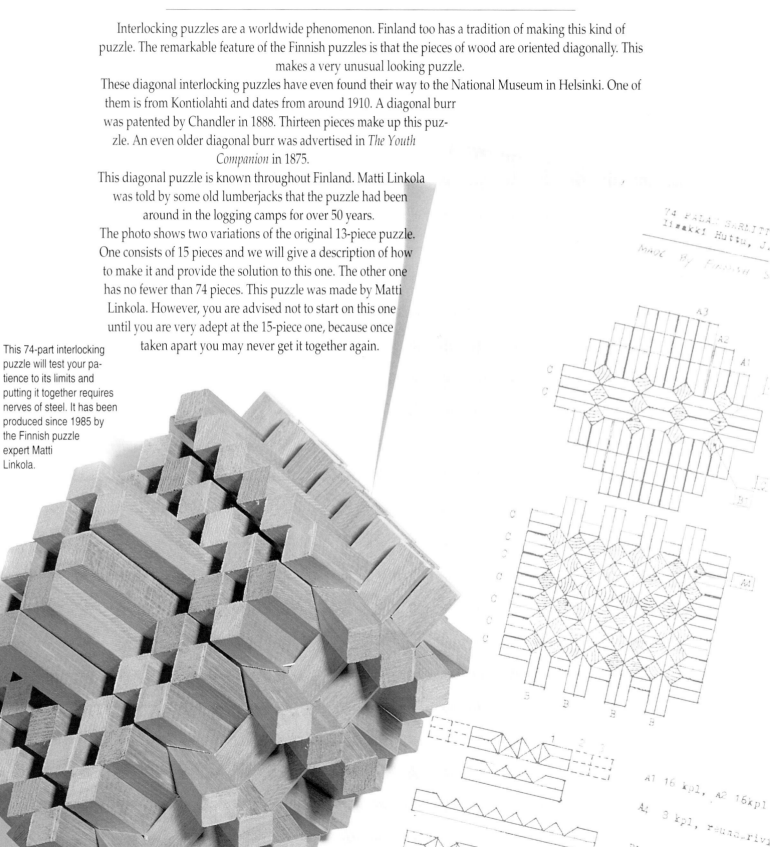

HOW TO MAKE THE 15-PIECE DIAGONAL BURR

For this you need fifteen 1⁄2 x 1⁄2 in. (10 x 10 mm) pieces of wood of 21⁄2 in. (65 mm) long. The diagram shows you how to cut the notches. You will see that these must be sawed at an angle. The notches are at a 45° angle to the long axis of the piece of wood. This notch requires precision because the pieces cross each other in three directions. Smooth the pieces really well with a file. To get the pieces quite accurate does seem, and is in fact rather complicated. However, you can make a device to aid you. Take an extra piece of wood and saw it lengthwise diagonally in two. Glue the two halves on a board (see diagram). Put the pieces of wood to be sawed, between them.

This version of the 15-piece Finnish interlocking puzzle was made in 1984 by the Czech puzzlemaker Pavlovic. At that time the design was almost one hundred years old, for the patent dates from 1888.

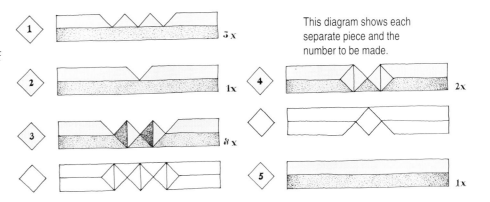

This diagram shows each separate piece and the number to be made.

1 — 3x
2 — 1x
3 — 8x
4 — 2x
5 — 1x

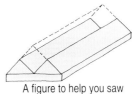

A figure to help you saw notches accurately.

SOLUTION

A. Put four pieces (no. 3) upright and insert one piece (no.1) through the lower notch.

B. Lay two pieces (no. 3) crosswise on piece no. 1 and insert another piece (no. 1) through the notch between these two.

C. Lay two pieces (no. 3) crosswise on pieces 3, 3 and 1 as in B and insert one piece (no. 1) through the middle.

D. Again add two pieces (no. 4) and one piece (no. 2).

E. Finally you insert the key piece (no. 5) through the remaining hole.

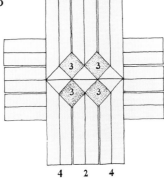

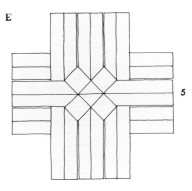

A RUSSIAN RATTLE BURR

Interlocking puzzles are often based on wood joints that were used for other purposes as well. The Japanese puzzles, for instance, are based on earthquake-proof architecture. The technique of the Finnish Diagonal puzzles can be recognized in log cabins.

In Russia, interlocking puzzles are also used as children's toys. On these pages you see a rattle made of two puzzles. The head piece consists of 24 pieces, and the tail piece of 6. Two of these pieces join the head and tail. In this toy the use of glue or nails is absent, just as in Japanese buildings. The head piece contains little pebbles to make the toy rattle.

The puzzle pieces can be cut from green wood and then assembled. Then, when the wood dries the puzzle shrinks slightly, the rattle fits more tightly and can be made to rattle noisily.

This Russian rattle from Russian puzzle designer and collector Anatoly Kalinin, consists of two parts: a 24-piece head and a 6-piece tail.

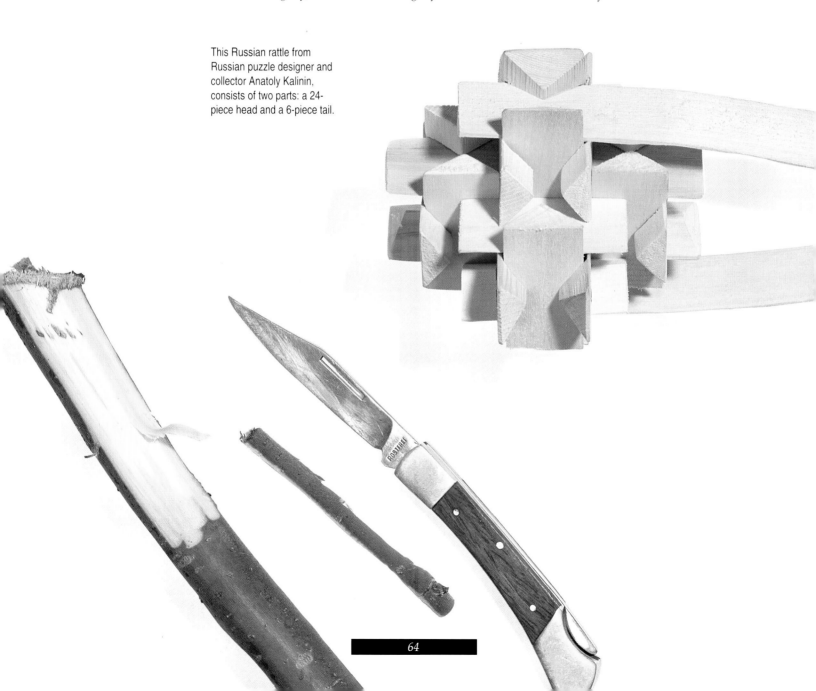

HOW TO MAKE A RATTLE BURR PUZZLE

You start by taking pine, willow or other soft wood. Using a knife whittle these into the puzzle pieces as shown in the diagram. It requires a certain degree of skill. Measurement A is the width of all the pieces and it should be used for all the notches as well. You should make the flat sides of the puzzle pieces as thin as possible, but not thinner than 1/16 in. (2 mm) per piece.

HOW TO ASSEMBLE THE PUZZLE

Start with the two handles C (16-17) and four pieces A, one with a notch. When assembled, these make the backside. First you place one piece on the bottom (1) between the handles and on top of this place two cross-pieces (2-3). Then wedge the final piece (4) between the notches. The top part with the marble or pebbles is assembled according to the numbers in the diagram. With the notched final piece (26) you lock everything together. After piece 20 the marble or pebbles should be put into the cavity. The numbers with arrows refer to the same pieces, but on the other side of the puzzle.

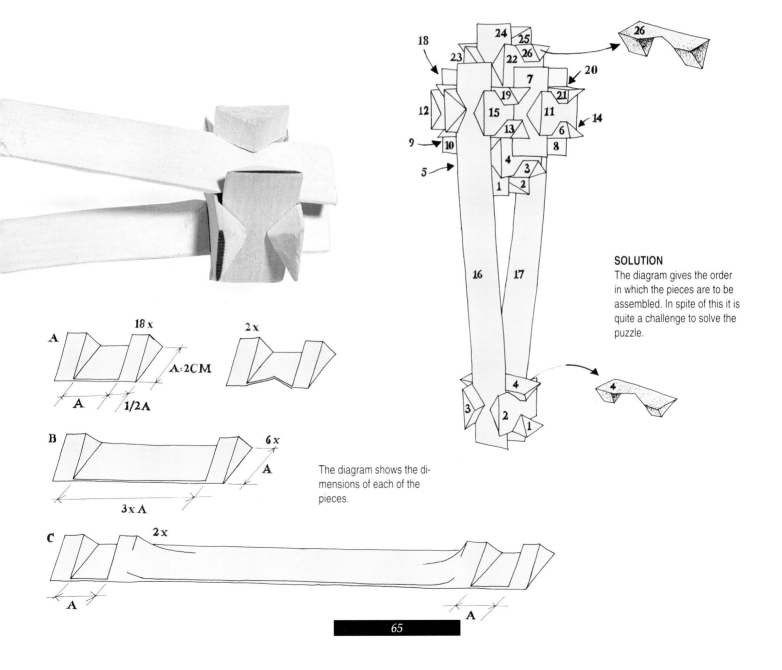

SOLUTION
The diagram gives the order in which the pieces are to be assembled. In spite of this it is quite a challenge to solve the puzzle.

The diagram shows the dimensions of each of the pieces.

THREE-DIMENSIONAL JIGSAW PUZZLES

The jigsaw puzzle is probably the best known mechanical puzzle in the world. From a very young age children learn to put loose pieces together to form an image. Jigsaw puzzles exist in numerous varieties, from very simple to extremely difficult, some with thousands of pieces.

In England, toward the latter part of the nineteenth century an additional dimension was added to jigsaw puzzles– literally, because at that time three-dimensional jigsaws of wood started to be made and sold. One version was patented in America in 1881. With the addition of a third dimension the degree of complexity was also increased; no longer were the pieces confined to a flat surface, they had to fit lengthwise, widthwise and depthwise into a solid shape. On these pages are three fine examples of three-dimensional jigsaw puzzles.

The Bantam Eggs three-dimensional puzzle dates originally from 1934, but the version shown here is from 1956. The puzzle was put on the market by Scrambled Eggs Inc. of Chicago. The first known three-dimensional puzzle was patented in America by McChesney in 1881.

The Dachshund Puzzle was used as an example for the make-it-yourself puzzle. The original was produced by Try-Lock and is just a bit more challenging.

This diagram gives the saw lines of Try-Lock's Dachshund Puzzle.

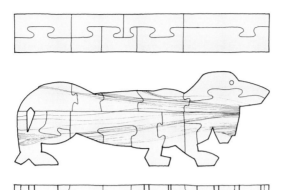

HOW TO MAKE A THREE-DIMENSIONAL JIGSAW PUZZLE

To make this puzzle you will need at least a very good fretsaw, but a jigsaw would be even better. In principle, any solid object can be transformed into a three-dimensional puzzle. Here we start from the dog shape in the photo and the diagram. To make an exact copy of this one you would need special equipment, so we'll give you a slightly simpler version.

Saw out the dog's outlines. Then saw the flat surface into a jigsaw pattern. Make sure there are enough projections to the pieces otherwise the puzzle will fall apart. Flush pieces don't stay together. Stick the pieces tightly together with gummed paper tape. Then turn the form on its side and saw another jigsaw pattern on this side. Do it carefully because the whole thing will be somewhat wiggly. You can use any pattern and make it as capricious as you like. But remember that the puzzle must still be workable.

Seasoned puzzlers can make it even more complex by taking the puzzle apart and cutting each piece in half again according to a jigsaw pattern. Putting this back together will keep you busy for awhile.

Wouldn't the heart make a nice Valentine?

"My heart, in several pieces see,
On bended knee I offer thee,
Broken – yes 'tis very true –
To make it whole is up to you."

With this little rhyme the Puzzle Guild Inc. of Chicago put this three-dimensional puzzle of a broken heart on the market. It was patented in 1902, but this specimen is from around 1930.

A Broken Heart

Trade Mark   U. S. Patent P.—Ser. No. 669866

A 3-Dimension Technisolid Puzzle

My heart, in several
pieces see
On bended knee I
offer thee,
Broken—yes 'tis
very true—
To make it whole
is up to you.

NOTE: The pieces in the box when properly assembled form a plump red heart. Each piece fits perfectly into its proper place. Some pieces slide into place in one direction only.
DO NOT FORCE PIECES!

Designed and Made only by
Puzzle Guild, Inc., Chicago
225 West Illinois Street

SOLUTION
The solution of the puzzle depends on your personal variation.

This diagram shows the reverse side of the dog.

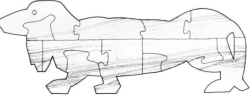

THE VIOLIN PUZZLES

This violin puzzle belongs to the group of wire, string and knot disentanglement puzzles. The objective is to disentangle one part, a ring or a handle, from another part and then to join them back together. These puzzles are made of various materials such as cast iron, sheet metal, wire and string: there are countless variations and some are quite difficult.

One of the most famous string puzzles was the Gordian Knot.

The story behind it: Gordius was a simple but exceptionally shrewd peasant. His shrewdness led him to become king of Phrygia. The legend tells us that Gordius, upon accepting the crown, tied his old clothes into such a knot that no one was able to untie it. The oracles of antiquity had revealed that whoever would loosen the knot would be the new emperor. Alexander the Great was among those who tried to untie the knot. When all his efforts remained unsuccessful, he became so enraged that he slashed the knot in two with his sword. The prophesies of the oracles came true: Alexander did become emperor.

The most widely told version goes like this though: In the temple of Gordium a horse's harness was tied to the pole of a wagon with an inextricable knot. The oracles divined: He, who can undo the knot will be ruler of an empire! In the year 333 B.C. Alexander the Great visited the temple and with a slash of his sword cut the knot in two. The divination came true – he became emperor. Even today, the saying cut the knot is reminiscent of this legendary faet.

This *Violin and Bow Puzzle* was created by Jean Claude Constantin of Germany. It is based on the 1904 Van Houten Tangled Violin Puzzle'.

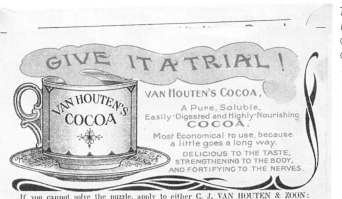

The Tangled Violin Puzzle is a fine example of an early twentieth century puzzle advertisement. It was made in 1904 by Jos. Vas Dias & Co. of Amsterdam for the Dutch Cocoa manufacturer Van Houten & Zoon. The puzzle, however, was produced in New York and Chicago and was intended for the American market.

HOW TO MAKE A TANGLED VIOLIN PUZZLE

On these pages two variations of the violin puzzle are shown. One antique advertising version is made of cardboard, the other is a miniature violin made of wood. We will show you how to make the cardboard violin. It is more complicated than the wooden violin, but we'll give the solution to both.

Trace the outline of the violin and the bow as shown on this page and transfer it onto cardboard. Cut out the violin. Then tie a piece of string to the violin as indicated in the diagram. Tie the second string to the bow and pull it through the loop of the violin. The diagram shows how to do it correctly.

To make it look more like a real violin you can paint or decorate it. Use plywood instead of cardboard for a more durable puzzle.

SOLUTION

The solution to both puzzles is similar, but the cardboard one is just a touch more difficult.

The diagram at the right gives the solution to the cardboard puzzle: the loop of the bow is pulled through the openings in the belly of the violin and the opening in the neck and looped around the end of the string in the neck. Pull the string back through the openings.

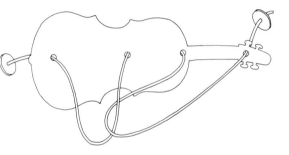

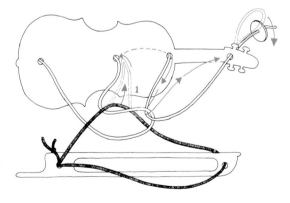

The diagram below shows the solution to the wooden violin puzzle.

It's more or less self-explanatory. Pull the string of the violin through the opening in the bow and loop it around the ring. The violin comes loose. Simple, isn't it?

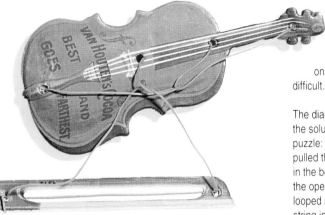

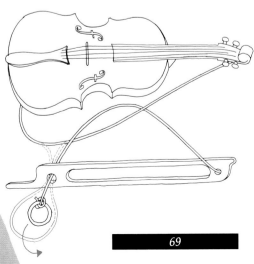

THE BUTTER NUT PUZZLE AND SPAGHETTI-EATER

Often it is very hard to pinpoint the time and place of a puzzle's birth. The principle for a puzzle sometimes is known long before the puzzle is commercially available, as in the case of the Japanese Kumikis.

In this photo you see two examples of puzzles that work on a principle that was mentioned as early as 1660 in the book *Secrets of Arts and Nature* by John Wecker. The objective is to separate the object at the end of the string from the other part.

The Butter Nut Puzzle by Schulze is a handsome example of an advertising puzzle from the early twentieth century. It is a color lithograph on cardboard of a little bakery boy carrying a large loaf of bread under his arm. The loaf is connected to the baker by a piece of string; the puzzle is to separate the loaf of bread without breaking the string. The Spaghetti-Eater is contemporary (1979), but works on the same principle.

The Butter Nut Puzzle was an advertisement for Schulze Bakery & Co. and it dates from the early twentieth century. But there are earlier records of similar puzzles. For instance in Ozanam's *Récréations Mathématiques et Physiques* from 1725.

The Spaghetti-Eater was created by Charlie Maiorana in 1979. The puzzle was produced by Charlie's Woodenworks Company in Washington, D.C. The puzzle is a disentanglement type. This puzzle concept is quite old; it was mentioned as far back as 1660 in John Wecker's *Secrets of Art and Nature*.

HOW TO MAKE THE BUTTER NUT PUZZLE

Use the puzzle in the picture as a model and trace it first on transparent paper, then transfer the tracing onto a piece of thin cardboard.

Make holes in the puzzle as indicated in the solution diagram. Then thread the string through the puzzle and attach the label to the end. Decorate it to your own taste.

The solution to both puzzles is similar.

HOW TO MAKE THE SPAGHETTI-EATER

Take a 3 1/8 x 7 7/8 in. (8 x 20 cm) piece of wood of 3/4 in. (2 cm) thick. Draw the figure of the spaghetti-eater in the illustration, or someone like him. Saw out the figure with a fretsaw.

To get the square opening in the belly start by drilling a small hole in one corner through which you can put the blade of the saw. Saw out the square and sandpaper the whole thing.

Then drill a 1/2 in. (12 mm) hole from the mouth to the square in the belly – a gullet as it were. Look closely at the diagram. Now drill two 1/4 in. (6 mm) holes through one side of the belly. The diagram gives the exact positions. Through these put two sticks of 2 3/4 in. (7 cm) long and 1/4 in. (6 mm) thick and fix them with glue. In the same side of the belly you drill another hole of 1/2 in. (12 mm) diameter. Smooth all the edges nicely.

Take a piece of cord, 6 1/2 ft (two meters) long and 1/8 in. (3 mm) thick and fold this in half. Thread it through one of the wooden balls (1 1/4 in. (3 cm) diam.) as shown in the photo. Glue the ball into the eater's mouth. Then thread the cord through the throat, around the two ribs and through the hole in the side of the belly. Finally you thread the two ends through the second ball and fasten them with glue. Now you can start taking it apart again.

Right: This diagram gives the shape and hole location for the Spaghetti-Eater.

SOLUTION

The solution to both the Butter Nut Puzzle and the Spaghetti-Eater is the same. Move the loop of the ball or the one behind the loaf along the cord, through the holes and joints, all the way to the other ball or, in the case of the bread puzzle, the label. Slide the loop around them and pull it back along the same way. Now the pieces of the puzzle should come apart.

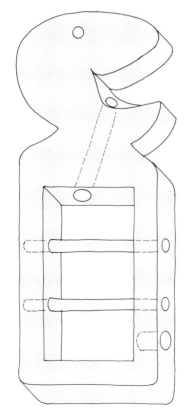

MOUSETRAPPING

These mouse puzzles also belong to the string or cord puzzle category. Two parts are connected by means of string. It is the puzzler's task to separate them.

These two mice are samples of the different materials that you can use in making puzzles. Wood is an excellent material, and so are paper and cardboard. But ceramic objects can be used very nicely in puzzles as well as shown by the mouse with the piece of cheese.

These puzzles are from Germany and the Netherlands. Although these two countries do not figure as prominently in this book as Japan and America, it does not mean that they don't have a puzzle culture. One of the authors of this book, Jack Botermans, is an absolute puzzle fiend. This wooden mouse puzzle is by none other than him.

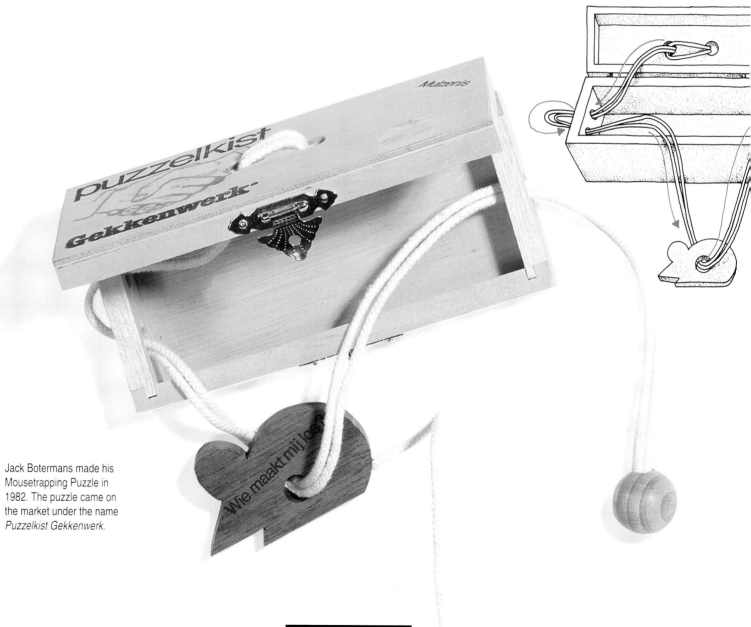

Jack Botermans made his Mousetrapping Puzzle in 1982. The puzzle came on the market under the name *Puzzelkist Gekkenwerk.*

HOW TO MAKE THE MOUSE IN THE BOX

The box is a regular standard box sold in most hobby stores. This model is 2¾ x 6 x 1⅝ in. (7 x 15 x 4 cm). In the box five holes are drilled with a ½ in. (1 cm) diameter drill bit. Two of the holes are in the lid, two in one short side, and one in the other short side.

The mouse is sawed out with a fretsaw from a 2¾ x 2 in. (7 x 5 cm) piece of dark wood ½ in. (1 cm) thick. In the middle a ½ in. (1 cm) hole is drilled.

You also need a 3¼ ft. (1 meter) long and ⅛ in. (3 mm) thick piece of cord. Fold this in half and put it through the holes in the lid. Now it should be put through the hole leaving a loop. You then pull the cord through the two holes in one side, then through the mouse and finally through the one hole in the other side. Glue the two ends in a wooden ball with a ¼ in. (6 mm) diameter hole in it. With a leftover end of cord you can give the mouse a tail.

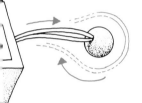

The diagrams showing the solutions can also be used as detailed instructions for making the puzzle.

HOW TO MAKE THE MOUSE WITH THE CHEESE

This model is made of baked clay, fireproof-clay to be precise. To make it you must have access to a kiln. Therefore, we recommend that you use self-drying clay which is sold in hobby stores.

Mold a mouse of around 2 x 2¾ in. (5 x 7 cm) and a piece of cheese of approximately the same size. Let your creativity run free. The mouse in the photo is just one example. You then fold a piece of cord of 3¼ ft. (1 meter) long in two, and stick the ends into the mouse's rear end. After they have dried you can paint the pieces with poster paint and varnish them to give them a ceramic look. When everything is dry you put the cord through the piece of cheese in the reverse order in which the solution is given in the diagram.

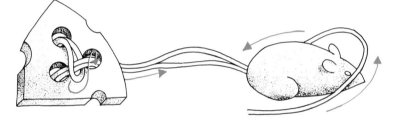

SOLUTION

Here too the solution is essentially the same for both puzzles: pull the end of the loop in the lid or the cheese back along the cord, through the holes and the mouse to the end of the cord to which the ball or the mouse is attached. Slide the loop around the ball or the mouse and pull it all the way through. If you've done it right the mouse should be free.

The Mouse and Cheese Puzzle is a relatively new puzzle. Jean-Claude Constantin of Germany made it just two years ago, in 1990. These puzzles are modern variations based on a principle that was published in a book by John Wecker in 1660.

WIT'S END

This cord puzzle can really drive you to despair. It consists of a wooden board with a wide and a narrow end. It also has a slot through which a cord is threaded. Both ends of the cord pass through a ring and end in two round beads which fit through the ring but not through the slot. Under the beads are two flat pieces of wood which in turn fit through the slot but not through the ring. And finally, the ring fits around the narrow end of the board but not around the wide end. Now what are you supposed to do? The ring has to come off the puzzle. No problem, or. . . It can be done though, even without breaking the board or cutting the cord. If you find this puzzle too easy, thread the cord through the slot twice.

This *Wit's End* is a very sophisticated disentanglement puzzle whereby one part fits through the slot but not through the ring, and the other part fits through the ring but not through the slot. Still, the ring can be separated from the cord.

HOW TO MAKE THE WIT'S END

Start with a wooden board of 10 5⁄8 x 1 1⁄4 in. (27 x 3 cm) and 1⁄8 in. (4-5 mm) thick, two beads of 5⁄8 in. (15 mm) diameter and a ring with a 1 3⁄8 in. (3.5 cm) diameter. In addition, a 15 3⁄4 in. (40 cm) piece of 1⁄8 in. (3 mm) cord is needed.

Saw the board with a fretsaw into a tapered form as shown in the diagram. Saw off the ends of the board to use as the flat pieces under the beads at the ends of the cord. Drill a 1⁄8 in. (3 mm) hole in both flat pieces.

The slot is sawed in the board with a fretsaw, after you have drilled a hole through which to stick the saw blade. Note: the slot should go past the spot where the ring gets stuck when the board is pushed through the ring. Smooth with sandpaper.

To keep it simple we start with the version in which the cord goes through the slot just once. Observe the diagram very carefully to see how the cord is threaded and the puzzle assembled. The more daring puzzlers among you might try the version in which the cord goes through the slot twice.

This diagram shows the solution to the simple version. The solution to the difficult puzzle is for you to discover.

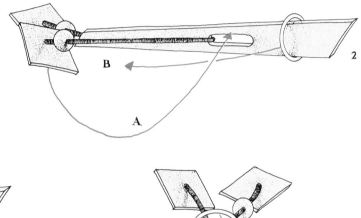

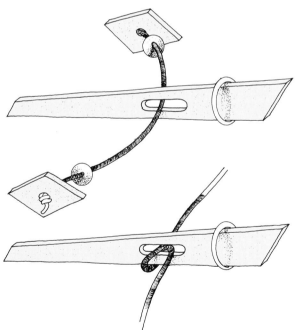

The diagrams on page 74 and above show the sizes and shapes of the different parts of the puzzle.
It is important that the ring be able to slide past the slot.

SOLUTION TO THE SIMPLE VERSION

Put the ring in its starting position, figure 1. Slide the ring around the end of the board and keep it behind the slot (1A). Put one flat piece through the slot (2A) and pull the ring back around the board and the one bead sitting against the slot (2B). Take the ring from the board and put it through the slot from the side with the two flat pieces (3B). The ring should now come free.

SOLUTION TO THE DIFFICULT VERSION

Now that we've given the simple solution, we think that the puzzlers might like to figure out the difficult version by themselves.
Still stumped?
Try it with the cord wound three times through the slot.

THE GORDIAN KNOT

Earlier in the book we spoke about the legend of the Gordian knot which was allegedly slashed in two by Alexander the Great in 333 B.C. The legend is bound to appeal to the imagination of many a puzzler – an inextricable knot. To create a puzzle that only the most expert puzzler can solve must be the ultimate dream of any puzzle designer.

The one shown here is a creation of one of the book's authors, Jack Botermans. The Gordian knot was his source of inspiration, and we ask you, the puzzler, whether you think he succeeded. Jack named his puzzle Gekkenwerk (the Dutch word lunacy), which says it all.

This model is made of cane, but there are also metal versions. If you want to make it yourself you had best use the pliable cane.

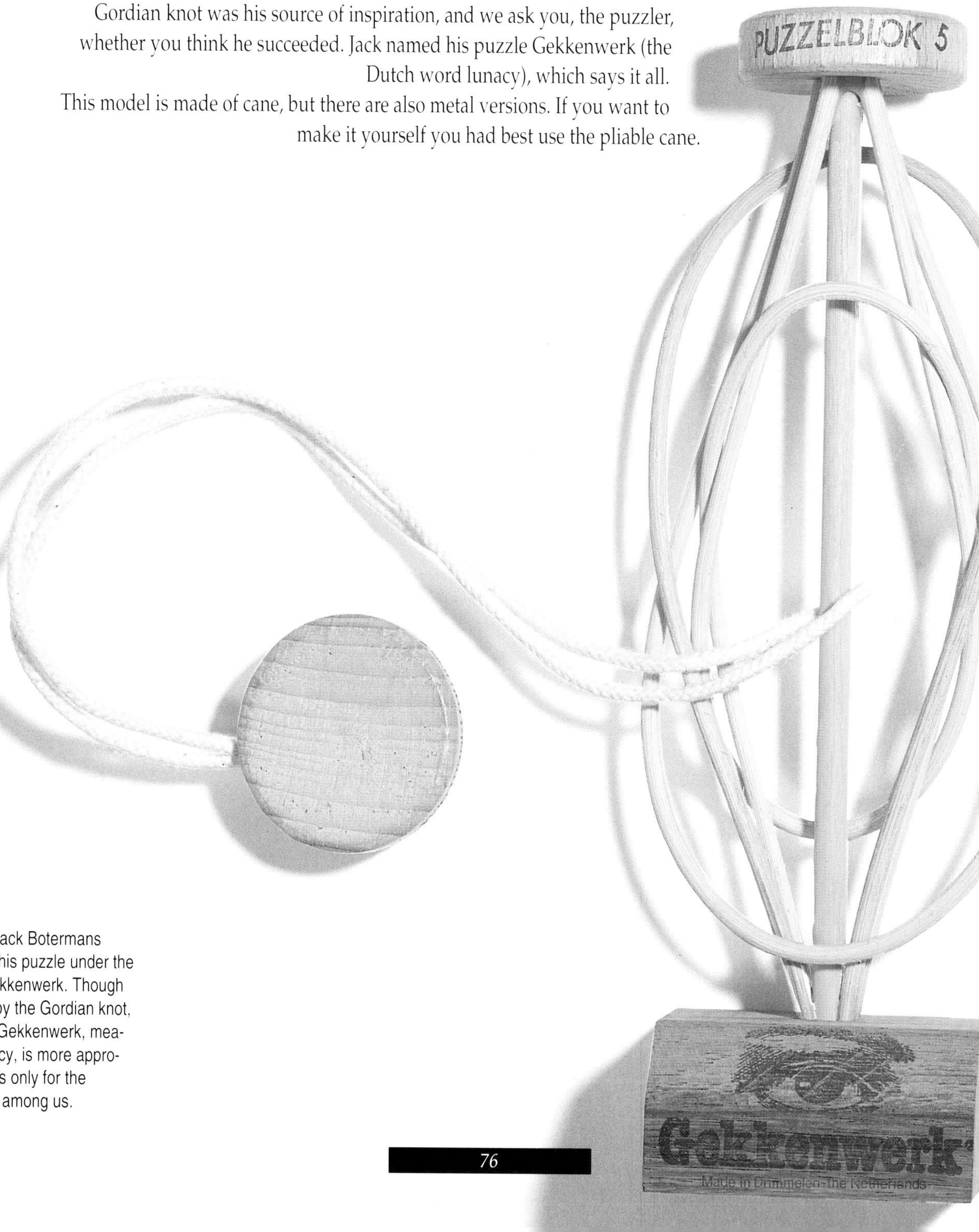

In 1983 Jack Botermans devised this puzzle under the name Gekkenwerk. Though inspired by the Gordian knot, the term Gekkenwerk, meaning lunacy, is more appropriate. It is only for the Einsteins among us.

HOW TO MAKE THIS GORDIAN KNOT

You will need:
1. Two lengths of cane 1/8 in. (3 mm) thick and 19⅝ in. (50 cm) long.
2. Two lengths of cane 1/8 in. (3 mm) thick and 15¾ in. (40 cm) long.
3. One stick 12 in. (30 cm) long 5/16 in. (8 mm) in diameter.
4. Two disks (of the old fashioned table shuffleboard type) or two wooden balls with a diameter of about 1¼ in. (3 cm).
5. One block of wood 2¾ x 3⅛ x 1⅝ in. (7 x 8 x 4 cm).
6. One length of 1/8 in. (3 mm) thick cord, 3¼ ft. (1 meter) long.

Thoroughly soak the cane in water. This will take about an hour. Meanwhile drill a 1/12 in. (12 mm) hole in the block of wood, the base, and one of the disks. Drill a 3/16 in. (5 mm) hole in the side of the other disk. When the cane is soft and pliable, take the two longer pieces and tie them in a thief knot. The diagram shows you how. Do the same with the shorter pieces. Then place one knot on top of the other and put the stick through both knots. Now put all the ends (4 x cane and 1 stick) into the glue-covered hole in the block of wood. Do the same at the other end with the disk. Tap it lightly with a hammer to fasten it in the hole. Study the photo carefully to see the location of the stick in relation to the knots. Lastly loop the cord around the central stick and glue the two ends in the side hole of the second disk. The only thing you have to do now is to take the disk with the cord away from the knot.

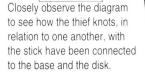

Closely observe the diagram to see how the thief knots, in relation to one another, with the stick have been connected to the base and the disk.

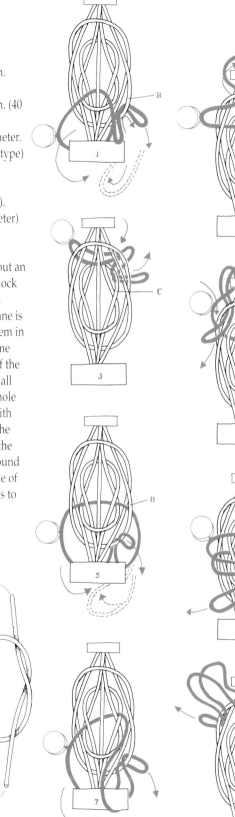

The diagrams show the step-by-step solution to the puzzle. By reversing the steps, you can put the puzzle back together again.

SOLUTION

First of all, place the puzzle in front of you exactly as shown in the diagram.

1. Move the loop along the bottom of the base and stick it through ring B. Move the loop back along the bottom of the base.

2. Now push the loop through ring A and move it over the top disk.

3. Push the loop front to back through ring C.

4. Move the loop back over the top disk and again push it through ring A.

5. Move the loop back along the bottom of the base and push it back to front through ring B. Move the loop back along the bottom of the base again.

6. Push the loop through ring D.

7. Now move the loop over the base through ring B.

8. Lastly, pull the loop through ring A and the cord comes free from the puzzle.

If you want to get the cord back in its original position after you have found a fellow victim, just start at solution step 8 and work your way back.

MAGIC HOLETITE PENCIL

The famous American puzzle inventor Sam Loyd was asked by the head of the New York Life Insurance Co., John McCall, to make an advertising puzzle that their salesmen could take with them, and that would make their clients remember its message. Loyd went home and returned to McCall the next day with a small stick attached to a loop of green cord. The stick looked like a policeman's billy club and it was slightly longer than the loop. McCall failed to be duly impressed. "What's the purpose of it?" he asked Loyd. Whereupon Loyd took McCall by his lapels, stuck the cord through the buttonhole and the stick in turn through the loop. "Alright," he said, "let's make a bet. If, within half an hour, you've gotten the stick out, without cutting the cord, I'll give you one dollar. If not, you owe me one." McCall pulled and pushed and, in short, spent 30 minutes of his valuable time trying in vain to remove the stick. After his time was up, Loyd accepted his dollar with the words: "In return for a $10,000 life insurance policy from NYLI, I'll take the thing right off of you!" Now McCall was impressed. "By this our clients will surely remember our salesmen!" The Buttonhole Puzzle became one of Loyd's most successful puzzles and it created the phrase "to buttonhole" someone.

The Buttonhole Puzzle, later sold as the Magic Holetite is one of Sam Loyd's most successful puzzles. Loyd's approach was that the simpler the puzzle appeared to be, the more people would want to have a go at it. Were they in for a surprise! The puzzle was advertising material for the New York Life Insurance Co. and was developed at the request of their general manager John A. McCall.

Our victim proudly wears the buttonhole pencil. After the photo was taken she attempted to remove the pencil, which afforded the photographer an amusing break. And, she may still be walking around with it attached.

MYST
YOUR FR

1. Place cord over thumb and fingers of right hand, as shown.

HOW TO MAKE THIS BUTTONHOLE PUZZLE

All you need is a pencil and a 12 in. (30 cm) piece of
string. In the bottom of the pencil you drill a small
hole in which you glue the piece of string folded in
two. Tie the ends into a knot and presto, you've
got your Buttonhole Puzzle.

HOW TO ATTACH THE PUZZLE

Follow the illustrations on the instruction sheet held by
our model, or rather victim in this case.

1. To get the pencil through the blouse, start by hanging
the string over thumb and fingers of your right hand. See
drawing.

2. Take the buttonhole with your right hand and move the
loop as far as possible past the buttonhole. In other words,
pull part of the blouse through the loop.

3. When a good part of the fabric has come through the
loop, you will see that the tip of the pencil will go through
the buttonhole fairly easily.

4. Pull the entire pencil through the buttonhole to tighten
the knot. Now, dare anyone to remove the pencil without
cutting the string or ripping the blouse!

MAGIC HOLETITE PEN
REG. U. S. PAT. OFF. 349,087
(Attach MAGIC HOLETITE Pencil
REG. U. S. PAT. OFF. 349,087
buttonhole, according to instructions p
Then dare anybody to remove it!)

...sp buttonhole between
...ers and thumb of right
...d; with left hand pull
...as far as possible past
...onhole, pulling coat
...gh loop of cord.

3. When loop is around quite
a lot of the coat material,
you'll find it is easy to put
writing end of the pencil
through the buttonhole.

4. To complete knot, pull pen-
cil through buttonhole.
SEE OTHER SIDE FOR
DIRECTIONS FOR RE-
MOVING PENCIL. ➞

Solutions in Chapter 8.

SOLUTIONS

The solution to each of the puzzles is the same. Move the loop at the end of the string along the string and through every hole towards the end with the button. Swing the loop around the button and pull the string back through the holes. The string plus button come free from the cardboard. The Untie-Puzzle needs a repetition of the last move and to complete the solution you have to untie the ring (3).

The diagrams show you how to attach the strings to the puzzles.

Délivrez mon Coeur is now the title of a song, but between 1900 and 1925 the title applied to a wooden puzzle by N. K. Atlas of Paris.

HOW TO MAKE THESE PUZZLES

These puzzles are all made in similar ways. The most convenient material is cardboard, but plywood or wood, as in the French heart puzzle, will do very nicely too. Trace the images and cut them out. Punch holes in the places indicated. We're not supposed to suggest this, but a color photocopy mounted on cardboard would be very handy. Photocopying is at odds with copyright laws, but if you are still reading this, the publisher has either over-looked it or doesn't mind terribly. (Our thanks to the publisher.) The diagrams show you how to attach the strings. To the ends you tie rings or buttons or whatever you have available.

These puzzles provide a lot of freedom to use your imagination to make your own variations, e.g. use a picture of yourself to make into a puzzle.

Of *The Chinaman Puzzle* only the manufacturer's name, Adams, is known. It was not used for advertising but was sold in shops.

TAKE THE
PIG-TAIL
OFF THE
CHINK

AUNT JEMIMA, UNTIE THE BEAR, THE PIG-TAIL OF THE CHINAMAN AND DÉLIVREZ MON COEUR

At the beginning of this century it became popular to advertise many products, whether flour, bread, shoes or clothing, through puzzles. The idea was that if a customer had to spend time solving a certain product puzzle, you could be sure that he or she would remember that particular brand. It was not without risk though. What if the customer was unable to solve the puzzle? He or she might never buy that brand again. Often the puzzles could be bought for a few pennies at a toy or candy store. Then they served another purpose: fun with learning for youngsters.

Aunt Jemima, Untie the Bear, The Pig-tail of the Chinaman and Délivrez mon coeur (The Captive Heart) are examples of this type of string puzzle. They are often made of cardboard and beautifully printed with color lithographs. Sometimes they're made of wood. The Captive Heart is a fine example of this; the box is made of cardboard and almost more attractive than the puzzle itself.

The principle behind this string puzzle is much older. It is mentioned as far back as the seventeenth century. And in the eighteenth century these puzzles were also well-known. In Ozanam's *Récréations Mathématiques* from 1725 these puzzles are described in detail.

We know a little more about *The Untie the Bear Puzzle*. It was put on the market by C. Schlindler of Toledo in 1909. Patent was applied for on May 2nd of that year.

The Aunt Jemima Puzzle advertises pancake mix made by R. T. Davis Mill Co. of St. Joseph. We don't know whether Aunt Jemima's smile concerns the quality of the mix or the poor puzzler who can't get her untied.

THE BRAIDED LEATHER PUZZLE

A braid is no big deal. Braiding is as old as man. It is a technique for making a number of thin strips into something strong. Rope, mats, leather belts and hair have all been braided. Most of these braiding techniques are still used all over the world. It's natural really. Or is it?

Martin Gardner, a world famous expert and author on mathematical games, wrote an article in *Scientific American* about the mathematical aspects of braiding. And he is not the only one who has studied braiding. In his article he mentions a number of well-known mathematicians who have been fascinated by the braid. One of these is the Danish poet, writer and mathematician Piet Hein. He used the theory of braiding to develop a game in which three threads were braided while all the ends were tied together. He did this as follows. Cut a piece of cardboard into the shape of a coat-of-arms shield and mark one side with an X. Punch three holes in it onto which you tie three strings, each 26 in. (66 cm) in length. Tie the other ends of the strings onto a solid object such as the back of a chair. You now find that you can rotate the coat-of-arms shield in 6 different directions, each different rotation will lead to a different braid. For example, you can twist the shield forward between the first or the last two strings etc. Two people can also play this game. In that case you make two coat-of-arms

In 1988 Jim Riley of Julian, California made this *Woven Leather Puzzle*. It really consists of two problems. How do you braid the leather band like that? And how do you get the string out of the braid?

The diagram shows the leather strip before braiding.

shields. Stretch the strings between them. Sit opposite one another and begin to make a braid while the other person unbraids the other side! Who is fastest?

This page shows an illustration of a braided puzzle. There are two problems to solve. First how is the braid made; then, how do you get the string off the leather piece?

HOW TO MAKE THIS PUZZLE

What you need. A leather strip 2 in. (5 cm) wide and 10 in. (25 cm) long. First of all you cut 5 notches along the length of the strip. The diagram shows you how to do this. Then you cut a hole 1/2 in. (10 mm) in diameter in one of the ends.

Now you weave the strip as described in the introduction, by twisting one of the ends between the strands. The diagram will help you.

When you have made a nice braid you stick the string through the hole, then through one of the strands of the braid and back through the hole again. Thread a bead with a diameter of just over 1/2 in. (1 cm) onto each end of the string. The puzzle is now ready. Are you going to take it apart again?

The diagram shows the solution for removing the string. Quite simple as you can see. However, you'll find the braiding more difficult.

SOLUTION
The solution for removing the string with the beads is as follows. Bring the cord in position as shown in the diagram. You push the leather

strip A through the hole so that a leather loop is made at the back of the braid. Then you can pull the string out of the loop. This is a very difficult puzzle for many people. The braiding is shown in Chapter 8.

THE SUPER SLEEPER-STOPPER

This puzzle belongs to the group of topological puzzles and was designed by Stewart Coffin in 1972. The purpose of The Super Sleeper-Stopper is as follows. The ball has to be taken to the loop on the other side of the block of wood. This is an excellent disentanglement puzzle without any tricks. The knot in the cord in the block of wood is glued tight. Concentration, patience and perseverence are needed to solve this puzzle.

HOW TO MAKE THIS PUZZLE

The puzzle has two holes in a wooden block measuring 1⅝ x ¾ x 3⅛ in. (4 x 2 x 8 cm). The block is composed of three types of wood. There is only one ball attached to the leather cord because in this case, the ball has to be moved from one loop to the other.

Take a good look at the photo and the diagram to see how this puzzle is constructed.

The diagram gives you a better view of how the puzzle is constructed.

The Super Sleeper-Stopper was invented in 1972 by Stewart Coffin of Lincoln, MA. Coffin's firm Ap-Art made the puzzle and put it on the market together with an instruction sheet which, incidentally, did not give the solution. The puzzle is also described in detail in Coffin's *Puzzle Craft* published in 1985.

The solution is shown in the diagram. By the way, the solution to the Super Sleeper-Stopper can be seen from the side.

SOLUTION

1. Push the ball through the loop at the front (1A).
2. Then pull the leather strip at the rear of the block backward so that the loop through which you have just pushed the ball, comes out at the back. (1B).
3. Now pull this forward again through the topmost hole (1C).
4. When the loop is back at the front, lying in front of the topmost hole, push the ball through this loop (2A).
5. Then pull the whole thing through the topmost hole again toward the rear (2B).
6. Finally, pull the leather strip back through the bottom hole toward the front (2C).

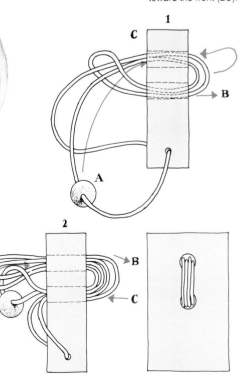

THE HORSESHOE PUZZLE

That the strangest things are used to make puzzles has become clear in this book. But horseshoes do not usually come to mind when you think of puzzles. To make this puzzle you have to be able to weld iron. The puzzle in the photo is based on a puzzle which was shown in Hoffmann's book *Puzzles Old and New* published in 1893 and is called Double Bow and Ring. Since then the puzzle has been included in many catalogs and in boxes of puzzles and puzzle sets.

Many stamped steel versions of these horseshoe puzzles have come onto the market. Most of them came from the U.S.A. and were stamped with advertising on the faces of the horseshoe.

Very recently a three-part variation of the horseshoe puzzle has been invented. In this version three central rings have to be removed instead of the third horseshoe.

This example of *The Horse-shoe Puzzle* was made in 1977 by Butch Ackerman of Fountain Valley, Calif. However, the design of the puzzle is actually much older.

The *Double Bow and Ring Puzzle* published in Hoffmann's *Puzzles Old and New* in 1893 is the same basic puzzle.

HOW TO MAKE A HORSESHOE PUZZLE

You need three horseshoes and two pieces of chain, each with three links.

Using a welder, join two horseshoes together with the chains. The diagram will show you how it should be done. Hold the third horseshoe over a gas flame until it is red hot. Then hammer it into an oval shape with a heavy hammer. You can weld the two ends together, but it isn't really necessary. The chances that you will bend open the iron horseshoe are pretty small. The two ends must touch one another.

To assemble the puzzle you just follow the steps shown for the solution in reverse.

The Triple Horseshoe Puzzle is a variation of the Horseshoe Puzzle. It was designed and made in 1991 by Jean Claude Constantin, a German puzzle maker whose puzzles have appeared elsewhere in this book.

The diagram shows the solution to this clever piece of ironwork, which once again only goes to show that muscles aren't everything. In this case brains are better!

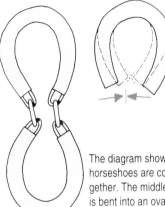

The diagram shows how the horseshoes are connected together. The middle horseshoe is bent into an oval shape.

SOLUTION

Take the puzzle in both hands. The closed iron is in the middle. Fold the puzzle in half, but in such a way that the two irons do not lie flat on top of one another but with a small angle between them. Pull the closed horseshoe up and slip it over one end of the horseshoes with the chain. Then allow the closed iron to drop down between the two ends of the open horseshoes. Slide the welded horseshoes directly on top of each other and slide the closed iron off. Study the diagram carefully if you have any trouble.

BOX OF WIRE PUZZLES

This box contains four different wire puzzles. The box comes from Germany and dates from about 1915. At least that was the year it was mentioned in the catalog of the Bartl Academy. German wire puzzles are usually made from thick wire, and are therefore often well-preserved. French puzzles on the other hand, are usually made from much thinner wire which rusts more easily. However, the German packaging is far less attractive than the French boxes with their beautiful lithographs.

Wire puzzles are of course highly suitable for making at home. You can also use a better and longer lasting material than ordinary wire. Silver wire and chrome-plated wire are excellent choices. For example, you could make a small wire puzzle from silver wire to wear as an earring or as another type of jewelry.

This box with four different wire puzzles comes from Germany. This puzzle was first mentioned in the catalog of the Bartl Academy in 1915.

SOLUTION
Fold the puzzle in half and with the pieces alongside each other, pull the ring over one of the hinges. Study the diagram. Pull the ring down in the puzzle shape. (See solution to the Horseshoe Puzzle).

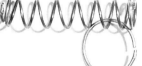

SOLUTION
Twist the ring half a turn and then pull it over the spiral.

SOLUTION
Push the oval through the eye of the puzzle and pull the oval round the spiral and back through the eye.

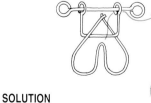

SOLUTION
Stick the indentation in the heart through a loop of the trapeze and then pull it over the end of the crossbar and back out again.

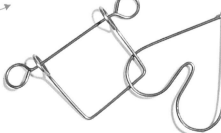

LA BALANCE DE THEMIS

Another very popular type of disentanglement puzzle is the wire puzzle. Wire puzzles have been around for many centuries. The wire puzzle, called Chinese Rings was, according to legend, invented in China in the second century A. D. It was used for mental training; disentangling such puzzles was regarded as an intelligence training exercise.

The so-called nail puzzles, whereby nails have been bent and twisted around one another, which then are to be disentangled, is a very common wire puzzle today. Wire puzzles have remained popular as entertainment and have been used as a sort of intelligence test. Albert Einstein was a fan, so was the American writer Jack London. Wire puzzles have been produced in Germany, France and England since about 1880. The puzzles themselves are often fairly simple and in plain boxes. In contrast, the packaging, especially in France, is often beautifully decorated with colored lithographs. The Balance de Themis pictured here is a fine example.

HOW TO MAKE THESE WIRE PUZZLES

Depending on your level of skill, various types of wire puzzles can be made. The simplest are made using a pair of pliers and special jewelry wire (silver wire) with a thickness of 1/16 in. (1.5 mm).

You can twist excellent eyes and bend the wire into fine curls using needle-nosed pliers. Rings can be made by winding a piece of wire round a stick and then sawing them through along the length of the stick.

If you want to make the puzzles from thicker material, use welding wire. This is available in various thicknesses at the hardware store. If you want to use wire thicker than 1/8 in. (3mm), you have to heat the wire first with a gas torch. Then clamp a piece of pipe in a vise and bend the wire round the pipe to make the rings.

It is important to adhere to the size proportions in each puzzle. They only work correctly if the proportions are followed accurately.

Use the models in the photos as examples when you make your own wire puzzles.

La Balance de Themis was put on the market between 1900 and 1925 by N. K. Atlas of Paris. This manufacturer has appeared several times in this book, for example with the Délivrez mon Coeur Puzzle.

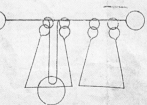

LES BALANCES DE THÉMIS

Amenez un des plateaux le long de la flèche en faisant glisser ses anneaux de cha-que côté et vous enlevez l'anneau de cuivre avec facilité.

Pour le remettre en place même opération.

6945

SOLUTION
Lay one of the U-shapes flat against the notch in the cross thread and pull the ring alongside the U-shape and this notch until it breaks free from the puzzle. See the diagram in the photo.

THE BURNING BOTTLE

In 1725 the book *Récréations Mathématiques et Physiques* by Ozanam was published. It had illustrations of a wire puzzle called the Chinese Ring Puzzle. Early examples of this puzzle were often made of wire, seven ivory rings and a beautifully carved ivory handle. Parts of this puzzle are still found in antique shops from time to time. Occasionally one can find a complete puzzle, which makes it a rare and valuable collectors item. In the nineteenth and early twentieth century a great many wire puzzles came on the market. If you search for them you may discover one in antique shops, at flea markets or auctions. Unfortunately the problem of finding incomplete Chinese wire puzzles also occurs with puzzles from Europe or America– that is, they consist of a number of small parts that easily get lost. So often when you think you've found a nice puzzle, you open the box and find that some, if not all, of the pieces are missing. The boxes especially the French ones are themselves very beautiful but of course it is much more rewarding and desirable to have a complete puzzle inside.

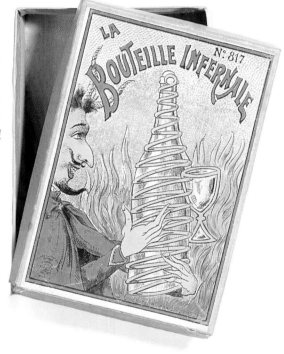

Missing pieces often make it difficult to reconstruct the original puzzle. In the case of the Burning Bottle, one of the puzzles on this page, we don't know what the position of the glass was originally in relation to the bottle, nor how the bottom loop and eyes were connected. So that becomes the puzzle: how was the Burning Bottle constructed? If you can discover that, you can surely take it apart again!

HOW TO MAKE THE BURNING BOTTLE

As we've said, you will have to find out exactly the right construction yourself. To make the bottle, use thin wire and a pair of needle-nosed pliers. Shape the wire after the model in the photo. Look at the illustration on the lid of the box to see how the glass is connected to the bottle. Good luck!

SOLUTION
The problem in this case is not the obvious question of how to separate the glass from the bottle, but how this puzzle was originally made? We will give you the solution to how you can get the glass off the bottle.
Wind the glass all the way up along the spiral, over the top and a little way down. Give the glass a half turn and you can free it from the bottle. But then again whether this solution works depends on how you attached the glass to the bottle in the first place.

A puzzle similar to La Bouteille Infernale was invented and patented in 1874 by Adolph Magerhaus. Before 1904 the puzzle was sold by the French firm S. C. (Editeur). The example shown here dates from the same time.

LES TRACAS DE L'ARTILLEUR

The man on the artillery shell looks like a modern version of Baron Munchausen, but that is not what this is about, although the Baron probably also wore a saber while flying around on his cannonball. This exceptionally well-preserved puzzle is about a saber which has to be freed from a wire

form consisting of squares. If this artilleryman is indeed to charge, he will have to get his saber first. With this puzzle comes a piece of paper with the solution. Originally most of these wire puzzles must have had the solution with them, but often they are missing. That's what makes this Tracas de l'Artilleur so special: the puzzle is complete, the box undamaged and the solution included.

The soldier's dress, as you can see on the box, indicates that this puzzle dates from World War I. It was initially put on the market in 1915 by Les Jeux Réunis, LJR. It was sold till after World War II, but production ceased in 1946. There was no longer a market for war puzzles.

SOLUTION

The folding sheet holds the solution to this puzzle. Push the saber through the ring and move it around the square ends of the other piece. Pull it back and the saber comes free.

HOW TO MAKE THIS PUZZLE

You can see that with most wire puzzles it is essential that the dimensions and shapes of the different pieces are correct relative to one another. For example the blade of the saber must fit through the ring and be long enough to go around the end of the other shape. When made of silver wire this puzzle makes a nice brooch to go on a jacket or blouse.

BLOOD, SWEAT AND TEARS

Wire puzzles literally come in every shape and size. By the end of the last century manufacturers capitalized on events or new fashions by producing another new puzzle. This wasn't difficult since many puzzles are based on the same principles. By altering the shape it appeared as though a new puzzle was born, while in fact the solution was practically the same. The packaging was a major factor in the puzzles' popularity. The color lithographs on the lid gave an impression of what the puzzle was about. A divorce for example is not easily recognizable in a couple of wire forms.

On these pages you can see some excellent examples of these wire puzzles. Le Cavalier et son Sabre is all but an exact copy of the Les Tracas de l'Artilleur Puzzle, and from the same manufacturer, Les Jeux Réunis of France. The pictures on the box are not the same so that it seems as if they are two different puzzles. When this puzzle first appeared in 1915, World War I was just one year old and the mood was still optimistic. Many manufacturers seized on the patriotic sentiments of the French by producing items adorned with the French flag and colors. And the puzzle producers' contribution was this type of soldier puzzle: an artilleryman for some and a cavalryman for others.

HOW TO MAKE THESE PUZZLES

As we have described earlier, these puzzles can best be made with wire and needle-nosed pliers. The Captured Chinamen Puzzle, however, can be made of much heavier wire such as 1/16 in. (2 mm) wire. This makes them less fragile and easier to handle. Do not use wire that is too thick because then you'll need a torch to heat the wire and special pliers to work it.

The box of Le Petit Porte-Veine shows us a pitifully weeping piglet with a big ax in its side. It was the puzzler's task to remove this murderous weapon. The puzzle is one from the line by S. C. (Editeur) of Paris and dates from before 1904.

This puzzle is called Comment Nous Séparer, translated How to Separate Us. On the box two Chinese men are depicted who are stuck together in a kind of neck clamp. The figures of the puzzle are not clearly recognizable as such, but it had to have a name. It is

made of heavy wire and dates from around the turn of the century.

SOLUTION
On the folding sheets in the photos you'll find the illustrations of all the solutions needed to do the puzzles.

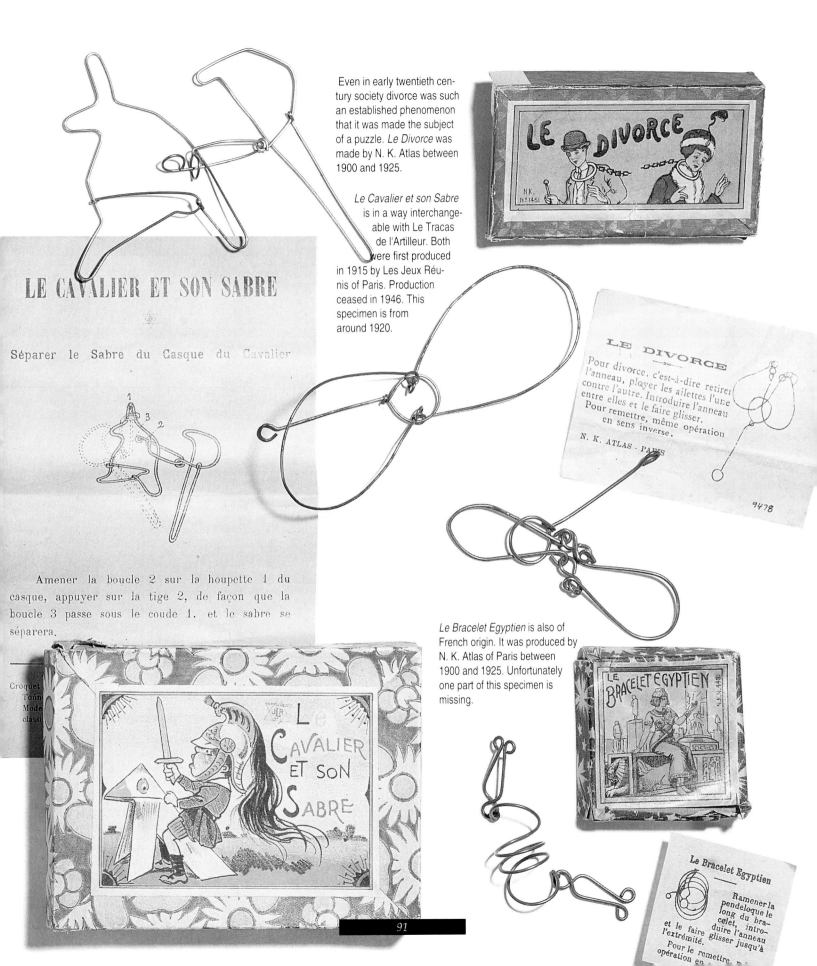

Even in early twentieth century society divorce was such an established phenomenon that it was made the subject of a puzzle. *Le Divorce* was made by N. K. Atlas between 1900 and 1925.

Le Cavalier et son Sabre is in a way interchangeable with Le Tracas de l'Artilleur. Both were first produced in 1915 by Les Jeux Réunis of Paris. Production ceased in 1946. This specimen is from around 1920.

LE CAVALIER ET SON SABRE

Séparer le Sabre du Casque du Cavalier

Amener la boucle 2 sur la houpette 1 du casque, appuyer sur la tige 2, de façon que la boucle 3 passe sous le coude 1. et le sabre se séparera.

LE DIVORCE

Pour divorce, c'est-à-dire retirer l'anneau, ployer les ailettes l'une contre l'autre. Introduire l'anneau entre elles et le faire glisser. Pour remettre, même opération en sens inverse.

N. K. ATLAS - PARIS

9478

Le Bracelet Egyptien is also of French origin. It was produced by N. K. Atlas of Paris between 1900 and 1925. Unfortunately one part of this specimen is missing.

Le Bracelet Egyptien

Ramener la pendeloque le long du bracelet, introduire l'anneau et le faire glisser jusqu'à l'extrémité. Pour le remettre, opération en

HEARTBREAKER

Two samples of the excellent ironwork by Uncle's Puzzles-Heritage Forge of Maple Valley, Washington. These are solid-looking hearts indeed. Not an easy job to "break" them. If you decide to make them, we suggest you use a thinner wire. Thin wire (1/6 in. or 2 mm) is very pliable, so very suitable to make a sturdy puzzle. Although it does not look modern, for then you might expect chromium plated steel, it is still sold by Heritage Forge in Maple Valley where they are masters at the art of forging.

This Heartbreaker is a simple version of the Heart's Desire Puzzle. It seems impossible to separate these two close hearts. But what do you know, it can be done! Why not start with the Heart's Desire then go on to the Heartbreaker?

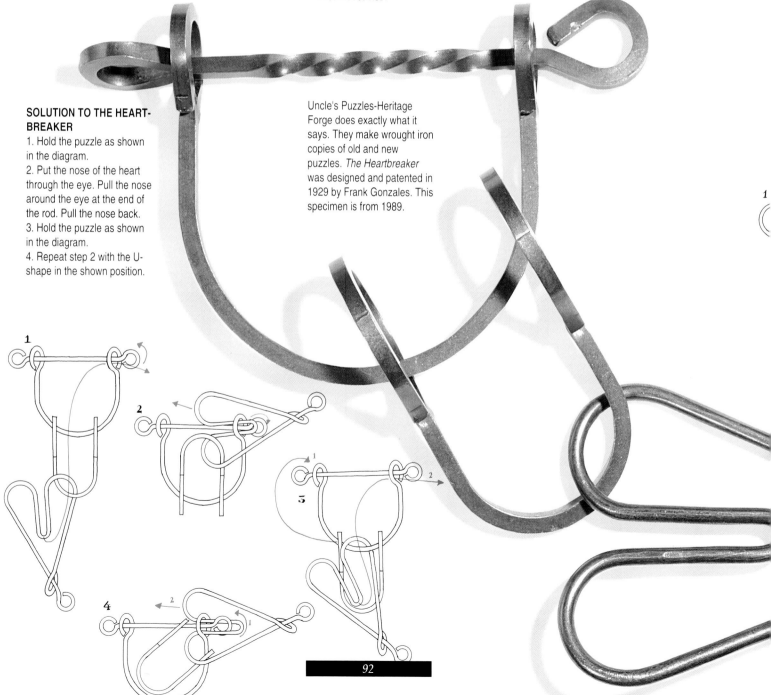

SOLUTION TO THE HEART-BREAKER

1. Hold the puzzle as shown in the diagram.
2. Put the nose of the heart through the eye. Pull the nose around the eye at the end of the rod. Pull the nose back.
3. Hold the puzzle as shown in the diagram.
4. Repeat step 2 with the U-shape in the shown position.

Uncle's Puzzles-Heritage Forge does exactly what it says. They make wrought iron copies of old and new puzzles. *The Heartbreaker* was designed and patented in 1929 by Frank Gonzales. This specimen is from 1989.

SOLUTION TO THE HEART'S DESIRE

1. Put the nose of one heart through the eye of the other. Slightly tip the first heart downward and slip the nose over the eye of the second heart. Observe the diagram carefully.

2. Now you only have to push the first heart up from the eye of the second, and you have two hearts whose heart's desire it is to be one. So quickly reunite them.

The Heart's Desire is another product of Uncle's Puzzles-Heritage Forge. The puzzle was shown and sold in the 1919 Johnson Smith Catalog. This specimen is from 1989 also.

HOW TO MAKE THE HEART PUZZLES

There's no escape. If you want to make the puzzle, you'll have to become a blacksmith. We suggest you use 3⁄16 in. (5 mm) welding wire suited for acetylene welding. Using a gas torch, heat the wire till it's red hot. Clamp a metal pipe of the desired diameter in a vise, and bend the wire around it. A monkey wrench is useful for holding the hot wire tightly against the pipe. With another pair of pliers you wind the wire round the pipe. We had our models chromium-plated for a splendid look.

This box is full of wire puzzles. It comes from Germany and was made in the thirties. Puzzles like these are the source of inspiration for Uncle's Puzzles-Heritage Forge.

GINGERBREAD MAN

Wire puzzles are not necessarily made of thin wire. On these pages are two more examples of puzzles made of wrought iron. This implies that not everybody can make one because it requires forging, i.e. the iron is heated until it is red hot and then bent and hammered into shape.

These two examples come from Uncle's Puzzles-Heritage Forge of Maple Valley, Washington. The Gingerbread Man gets its name due to its shape vaguely resembling a piece of gingerbread. But there the similarity ends. It's easy to pull a piece of bread apart, whereas this puzzle demands ingenuity, since muscle power won't get you anywhere. The objective is to remove the ring without using force.

HOW TO MAKE THESE PUZZLES

The average hobbyist will find it impossible to make them since a complete forge is needed. We advise making them of thinner wire, as described in previous puzzles, or buying them from Uncle's Puzzles-Heritage Forge in Maple Valley, Washington.

The Gingerbread Man, like the Fooler, is made in Maple Valley and dates from the same year. It is a little easier than its companion because there is no trick involved.

SOLUTION TO THE GINGERBREAD MAN

These puzzles work in fact along the same line as the horse-shoe puzzles. You fold the puzzle in two and slip the ring first over one end and then between the two ends. Next you move it downward along one side (which also has the triangle), and up along the other side. You can then slide it right off the puzzle. A good look at the diagram will help.

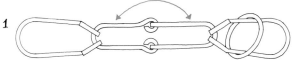

The Fooler is a piece of good old-fashioned ironwork. The puzzle was made in 1989 by Uncle's Puzzles-Heritage Forge in Maple Valley, Washington, but the basic design is much older. The puzzle was invented and patented by Bowen E. Clarkson in 1904.

FOOLER

This puzzle is a variation on the Gingerbread Man in that the ring must be removed. But the comment: "there's a little tom-foolery in this case. . .", may hold a clue to the solution. These puzzles are just what the doctor ordered for impatient puzzlers. If, in sheer frustration, you should want to rip your puzzle to pieces, these are the remedy. They're easier solved than destroyed.

SOLUTION TO THE FOOLER

1. Attention: the loose ring must be at the side of the U-form with the vertical eyes. Fold the puzzle in two at the middle hinge, in the direction in which the puzzle becomes the flattest, but without using force.

2. Slide the U-form (A) all the way up to the hinge point, allowing the ring to just go over one leg of the next U. Examine diagram.

3. Move the ring on to the left side. See diagram.

4. And now the unexpected move– the Fooler you might say. Push the upper U-form, with slight force, over the lower one, thus creating a double U.

5. By moving the ring in the direction of the arrow it will come right off.

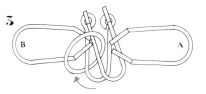

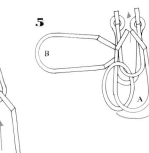

THE INDIANS AND TRAVELLERS PUZZLE

Presumably everybody knows the puzzle of the farmer, the wolf, the goat and the cabbage. He has to take the whole menagerie across the river, one at the time, but he can't leave the wolf with the goat, nor the goat with the cabbage because the former will eat the latter. The problem is how does he get them all to the other side when he can only take one at a time in his little boat?

This problem is very old. In the eighth century the erudite cleric Alcuin asked his pupils questions like these. Ten centuries later the citizens of Königsberg came up with a similar question: Can one cross all the bridges of the town without crossing a single one twice? A world-famous mathematician grappled with the problem and proved that this undertaking was impossible. In describing this he initiated a new discipline: topology.

Milton Bradley & Co. put a puzzle on the market by the end of the nineteenth century which contained a number of such problems. In the original puzzle three white travellers have captured three Indians. It can, of course, be the other way around.

5.

Sequential movement puzzles.
Objective: Moving parts of object to a goal is the puzzle.

Pages 96–115

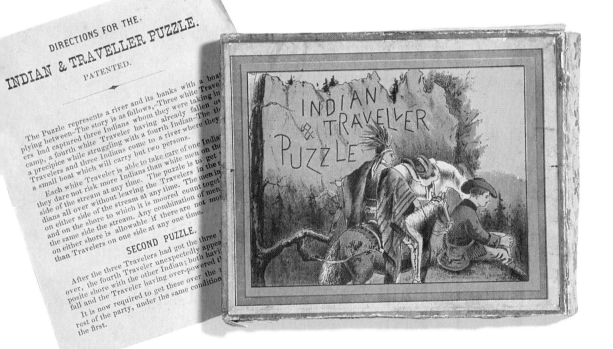

The Indians and Travellers Puzzle was produced by Milton Bradley & Co. It was one puzzle with several variatons included. Although it was known much earlier, the puzzle was patented in 1880 by S. J. Delan under the name Black vs White Men. Milton Bradley & Co. substituted Indians and husbands, etc. for black men.

DIRECTIONS FOR THE
INDIAN & TRAVELLER PUZZLE.
PATENTED.

The Puzzle represents a river and its banks with a boat plying between—The story is as follows, Three white Travellers had captured three Indians whom they were taking to camp, a fourth white Traveler having already fallen over a precipice while struggling with a fourth Indian—The three Travelers and three Indians come to a river where they find a small boat which will carry but two persons.

Each white Traveler is able to take care of one Indian, but they dare not risk more Indians than white men on the same side of the stream at any time. The puzzle is to get the Indians all over without leaving the Travelers in the minority on either side of the stream at any time. The men in the boat on the shore to which it is moored count together with the same side the stream. Any combination of men on either shore is allowable if there are not more Indians than Travelers on one side at any one time.

SECOND PUZZLE.

After the three Travelers had got the three Indians over, the fourth Traveler unexpectedly appeared on the opposite shore with the other Indian; both having escaped the fall and the Traveler having over-powered the Indian. It is now required to get these over the river to the rest of the party, under the same conditions as the first.

Solutions in Chapter 8.

INDIANS AND TRAVELLERS PUZZLE I

The puzzle depicts a river with a boat to cross the river. The story goes like this: three white travelers had captured three Indians and had taken them to their camp. A fourth white man has fallen into the water during his struggle with a fourth Indian. The former come to a river in which lies a small boat to get to the other side.

Each of the three white men can take one Indian with him in the boat to cross the river. But they dare not leave more Indians than white men on one bank. The question now is how to get all the Indians and all the white men across without ever leaving more Indians than white men on either side.

INDIANS AND TRAVELLERS PUZZLE II

After the white men have succeeded in getting all the Indians across, the fourth white man and Indian come along. And on the wrong side of the river of course. The second problem is: how do the white man and the Indian get across when the same conditions apply as in Puzzle I?

THE JEALOUS HUSBANDS III

Mark three of the travellers HA, HB and HC respectively.

Mark three of the Indians A, B and C. They now represent the wives. You are faced with the following problem: three couples are on one side of the river. They have to get across in a boat that only carries two. The husbands are so jealous though that they are loath to leave their wives in the company of the other husbands. How are you going to get all the couples to the other side without leaving any of the wives unchaperoned?

THE FOX, GOOSE AND CORN PUZZLE IV

The box also contains loose pieces representing the fox, the goose and the corn. One of the travellers is the farmer. This is in fact an American version of the Dutch farmer with the cabbage, goat and wolf. How does he get the fox, goose and corn to the other side without leaving the fox alone with the goose and the goose with the corn?

THE MEN AND BOYS PUZZLE V

Two men weigh 220 lbs. (100 kilos) each. Two boys each weigh 110 lbs. (50 kilos). All four of them have to get to the other side of the river in a boat that can only hold 220 lbs. (100 kilos). How do they get there without getting wet?

The diagram shows the configuration of the two river banks and the boat.

HOW TO MAKE THIS PUZZLE

This model is made of:
1. One piece of wood of 1⁄2 x 5⁄16 in. (12 x 8 mm), 3⁄16 in. (5 mm) thick.
2. Four bars of wood of 3⁄16 x 3⁄16 in. (5 x 5 mm), 3 1⁄8 in. (8 cm) long.
3. Two bars of wood of 1⁄2 x 3⁄16 in. (10 x 5 mm), 3 1⁄8 in. (8 cm) long.

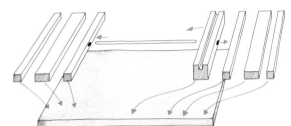

4. One bar of wood of 1⁄2 x 3⁄16 in. (12 x 5 mm), 2 in. (5 cm) long.
5. A plywood board of 4 x 8 in. (10 x 20 cm), 1⁄16 in. (2 mm) thick.
6. Metal wire of 2 3⁄4 in. (7 cm) long, 1⁄16 in. (1.5 mm) thick.

Piece 1 becomes the base on which the bars are glued with a space of 1⁄16 in. (2 mm) between them. On each side two bars of 3⁄16 in. (5 mm) and one bar of 1⁄2 in. (10 mm) wide (2 and 3). Before you fasten them, drill a 1⁄16 in. (1.5 mm) wide and 1⁄8 in. (4 mm) deep hole exactly in the center of two of the 3⁄16 in. (5 mm) bars. In these holes, put the wire along which the boat slides. The boat is made of bar # 4. Saw a 1⁄16 in. (2 mm) wide slot lengthwise in this bar, and through the side drill a hole of a little over 1⁄16 in. (1.5 mm).

Glue the whole thing together with the wire in the holes in the bars and through the boat.

The four men, the four Indians, and the images of the fox, the corn and the goose are sawed from the plywood. The diagram gives the shapes that you can use for the figures. Use a jigsaw and sandpaper the edges. Be sure that the glue has dried completely before placing the figures in the puzzle or they'll get stuck. Now see who gets who to the other side.

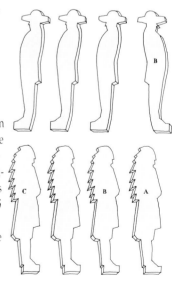

You can experiment with the variations of figures of the men, Indians, fox, goose and corn if you wish.

DOUBLE FIVE PUZZLE

In 1859, the English magazine *Indoor and Outdoor,* published an article about a puzzle that is similar to the Double Five Puzzle. The Double Five Puzzle consists of a circle with ten holes and ten disks. The objective was to group the ten disks in five equal stacks, spaced evenly. This may not look difficult, but with every move a disk had to jump two other disks, whether single or stacked. A stack cannot have more than two disks and each disk can only be moved once.

That makes it a more difficult puzzle.

The Double Five Puzzle probably originated in England. A
similar puzzle was published
in the English magazine
Indoor and Outdoor in 1859. A
year later it appeared in the
Boys' Own Conjuring Book.
(1860).

HOW TO MAKE
THE DOUBLE FIVE PUZZLE

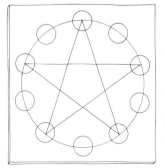

It would be great if you could also have such a nice box to
keep your puzzle in. But really all you need for the puzzle is
this: ten checkers, a piece of cardboard and a pencil or pen.
Draw a circle with a 6 in. (15 cm) diameter and divide the
line into ten equal lengths. You can use the star shape in the
diagram.(To explain how a pentagon is constructed goes a
little too far we think.) Trace the star on transparent paper;
on each point draw a circle the size of a checker. The star in
the middle makes puzzling easier.

Left: The star simplifies
dividing the circle into ten
equal parts.

Solution in Chapter 8

THE GREAT 13 PUZZLE

Another type of puzzle that many of you will be familiar with is the solitaire puzzle. It comes in many forms and sizes and is sold everywhere. We know that even around 1700 there were solitaire puzzles. An engraving by Jean Claude Berey from 1697 shows a French 37-hole board. By the end of the last and the beginning of this century there was an enormous puzzle boom. Thousands of kinds of puzzles appeared. As you may have noticed, many of the puzzles shown in this book are from that period.

Among them the Great 13 Puzzle by W.C. Breitenbach. This solitaire version, allowing diagonal moves, was patented and marketed in 1889. The marbles have to be removed by jumping and the puzzle is solved when one marble is left in the center.

In 1985 a book by John Beasley was published called *The Ins and Outs of Peg Solitaire* in which he describes and analyzes many forms of solitaire.

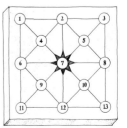

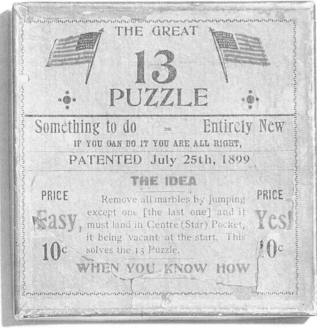

The Great 13 Puzzle is a variation of the original solitaire puzzle which was known in the seventeenth century. This version, developed by W. C. Breitenbach, U.S.A, was patented July 25th, 1899.

HOW TO MAKE THIS SOLITAIRE PUZZLE

For the base you need a 4 x 4 in. (10 x 10 cm) piece of wood, ½ in. (1 cm) thick and in addition 12 marbles to play with. On the wood you draw the pattern given in the diagram. At the points where the lines cross, bore holes with a diameter corresponding to that of the marbles. Don't drill too deep, for the marbles must be able to be picked up easily. Trace the pattern in ink on the board and finish it with paint and varnish.

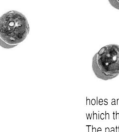

Solution in Chapter 8

The pattern shows the positions of the holes and the directions in which the marbles are moved. The pattern must be copied on the board.

SOLITAIRE

The English 33-hole solitaire board is probably of German origin. In 1710 the puzzle emerged in a publication by Gottfried Wilhelm Leibnitz, who not only played the game of removing the pieces but invented all sorts of variations with geometrical designs. But solitaire is very likely much older.

The previously mentioned engraving by Berey indicates that the puzzle was known at the court of Louis XIV, but there are reasons to believe that even before that there were games/puzzles that were the basis for the later solitaire. However, the historical origin has yet to be documented or proven.

This form of solitaire has remained popular throughout the ages, and certainly is the most popular version today. It was shown in Bestelmeier's catalog in 1803 and since then has been sold by most game and toy stores.

The solitaire shown on this page was made in Germany in 1913 by J. W. S.+ S. and sold in America by Spear's Games.
The objective of this Solitaire Puzzle is to remove all the marbles except one, by jumping. The last marble must be in the center of the board. You can think up all kinds of variations, for example, remove the marbles by jumping and leave an area with a certain design.

The solitaire puzzle has been known in Europe since the seventeenth century. The specimen shown here dates from 1913 and was made by J. W. S.+ S. of Bavaria. The puzzle was put on the market by Spear's Games and it appeared in the Bestelmeier's Toy Catalog.

SOLUTION
As we've said earlier, there are many different ways in which to play on this solitaire board. In *Creative Puzzles of the World* by one of the authors of this book, 18 other solutions for solitaire are given on pages 170–173. We only provide the solution to the 33-hole solitaire in the final chapter of this book.

HOW TO MAKE THE SOLITAIRE BOARD

You need a 8 x 8 in. (20 x 20 cm) wooden board of 1/2 in. (1 cm) thick. Transfer the pattern in the diagram onto the board and bore shallow holes at the intersections in which the 32 marbles will go. Sandpaper the board till nice and smooth and finish it with oil or transparent lacquer.
The four black points at the corners of the cross of holes provide an alternative ("French") version of solitaire. For it you will need 36 instead of 32 marbles.

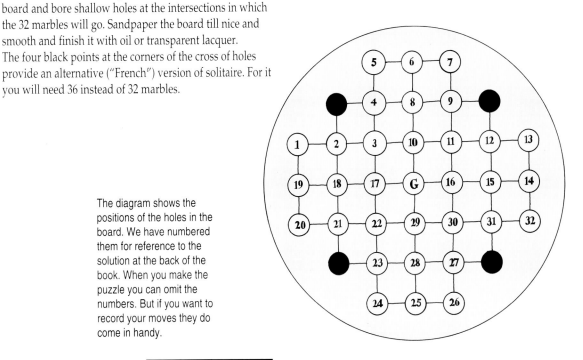

The diagram shows the positions of the holes in the board. We have numbered them for reference to the solution at the back of the book. When you make the puzzle you can omit the numbers. But if you want to record your moves they do come in handy.

THE TRIANGLE PUZZLE BOARD

On October 27, 1891, Herbert M. Smith was granted an American patent to a puzzle which he named the Triangle Puzzleboard. It is a variation on the solitaire puzzle described earlier.

The puzzle consisted of a wooden board with holes in a pattern of four triangles. Fifteen wooden pegs are placed in all the holes, with the exception of the central one. The objective is the same as in regular solitaire. By jumping the pegs you have to remove all but one and try to get the last one in the center of the board. The puzzle was kept in a cardboard box decorated with a picture of the puzzle.

The Triangle Puzzleboard is a variation on the solitaire puzzle described earlier in this book. On October 27, 1891, Herbert M. Smith was granted a patent for his design. John Beasley includes many triangular solitaire variations in his book *The Ins and Outs of Peg Solitaire.*

HOW TO MAKE THE PUZZLE

Take a 4 x 4 in. (10 x 10 cm) wooden board about 3⁄4 in. (2 cm) thick and copy the pattern as given in the diagram. At the points where the lines cross, bore 16 holes with a 3⁄16 in. (5 mm) diameter to a depth of 1⁄2 in. (1 cm). These will hold the pegs. The pegs are made of 1 in. (2.5 cm) long sticks with a 3⁄16 in. (5 mm) diameter. Sand the pegs nice and round to easily fit the holes. Smooth the board nicely too and finish it with paint and ink like Herbert M. Smith did, or with your own artistic design. You could also transfer the pattern onto a piece of paper and glue this onto the board. This, however, will make the puzzle more easily damaged than if you draw the pattern directly on the board.

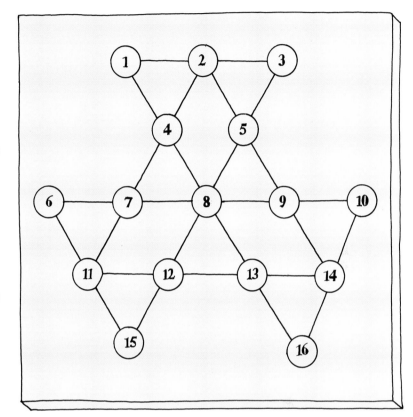

The diagram gives the pattern for the puzzle. The numbers are used in the solution at the back of this book.

Many historically famous names were given to the puzzles. This puzzlebox from the beginning of this century might explain why Napoleon lost the battle at Waterloo!

Solution in Chapter 8.

THE PYRAMIDS PUZZLE

This puzzle is the subject of various legends, particularly concerning its origin. In 1883 the French mathematician Edouard Lucas devised the puzzle and called it Tower of Hanoi (La Tour d'Hanoi). It consisted of three spikes set in a base; one of these spikes held eight wooden disks increasing in size from the top to the bottom one. The objective was to transfer this tower of disks to one of the other spikes, never allowing one disk to sit on another smaller than itself. Not impossible it seems. But the solution requires no less than 255 movements between the three spikes.

From the same period comes a myth regarding the puzzle's origin. It probably was fabricated by Lucas himself, who thereby gave his puzzle an air of mystique: The legend is that in the temple of Benares, where the center of the world lay, there was a brass plate on which stood three diamond needles. While creating the world, God placed 64 gold disks, from large to small, on one of these needles. This is the tower of Brahma. The priests, in accordance with the laws of Brahma, remove one disk at a time to one of the other needles. The disk on top of which the priest places his can never be smaller than the one going on top of it.

This *Pyramids* – A Problem from the Ancients is a newer version of the Tower of Hanoi that the Frenchman Lucas invented in 1883. This splendid puzzle was initially produced in 1929 for Knapp Electric Inc. of New York by the firm of Master Thinker. It appeared in the Johnson Smith Catalog of the same year.

In addition, only one disk at a time can be moved. Once the tower has been transferred from one needle to another, everything will turn to dust and the world come to an end with a big bang.

Not to worry though. To move these 64 disks from one needle to the other needle 18,446,744,073,709,551,615 movements are needed. So you can sleep peacefully.

The puzzle pictured here is a variation on the one by Lucas. The tower became a pyramid and the story is set in Egypt. The puzzle dates from 1929 and was made for a power company. Thank heaven they included a solution sheet in the box.

HOW TO MAKE THIS PYRAMIDS PUZZLE

You will need the following things:
1. A wooden board 6 x 6 x 1⁄2 in. (15 x 15 x 1 cm)
2. Three 2 in. (5 cm) long sticks 5⁄16 in. (8 mm) diameter
3. Eight round disks with a 3⁄8 in. (9 mm) hole in the center. The disks are 3⁄4, 15⁄16, 11⁄8, 11⁄4, 17⁄16, 11⁄2, 13⁄4 and 17⁄8 in. (20, 24, 28, 32, 36, 40, 44 and 48 mm) in diameter respectively.

The disks used in our model are 1⁄8 in. (4 mm) thick. Place the sticks in 5⁄16 in. (8 mm) holes in the board, in the shape of an equilateral triangle with 23⁄4 in. (7 cm) sides. The tips of the sticks are first sanded nice and round. If you want a real pyramid use square disks instead of round. This will get you a stepped pyramid.

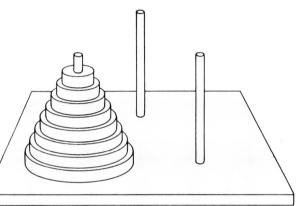

SOLUTION
At the back of this book is the solution as it was included in the box of the puzzle. Don't be in a hurry because it will take 255 steps to transfer the pyramid.

THE RAILROAD PUZZLE

A good example of a type of puzzle that was used for advertising purposes is the sliding piece puzzle. A variant with which we're all familiar is a square frame enclosing a number of blocks that, when you slide them correctly, result in a sequence of numbers or an image. A somewhat more complex type is the railroad shunting puzzle. These are puzzles in which a locomotive with some cars have to be moved in a groove from one side to another, thereby reversing the order of the cars. The track has a parallel double stretch, a siding, or sometimes a turning platform on which two cars or the locomotive with one car are placed to reverse the direction of the train. The first U.S. patent was issued to P. Protheroe in 1885 for a railway shunting puzzle. In this puzzle the cars were placed at random and with the help of the locomotive and the turning platform had to be arranged so that the letters on the pieces spelled the words Humpty Dumpty.

The Great Northern Puzzle was the most famous and popular railroad puzzle. It looks deceptively simple. The tracks form a triangle and the locomotive has only two cars. But there's more to it than meets the eye. Unfortunately an original copy of this puzzle from the last century has not yet turned up.

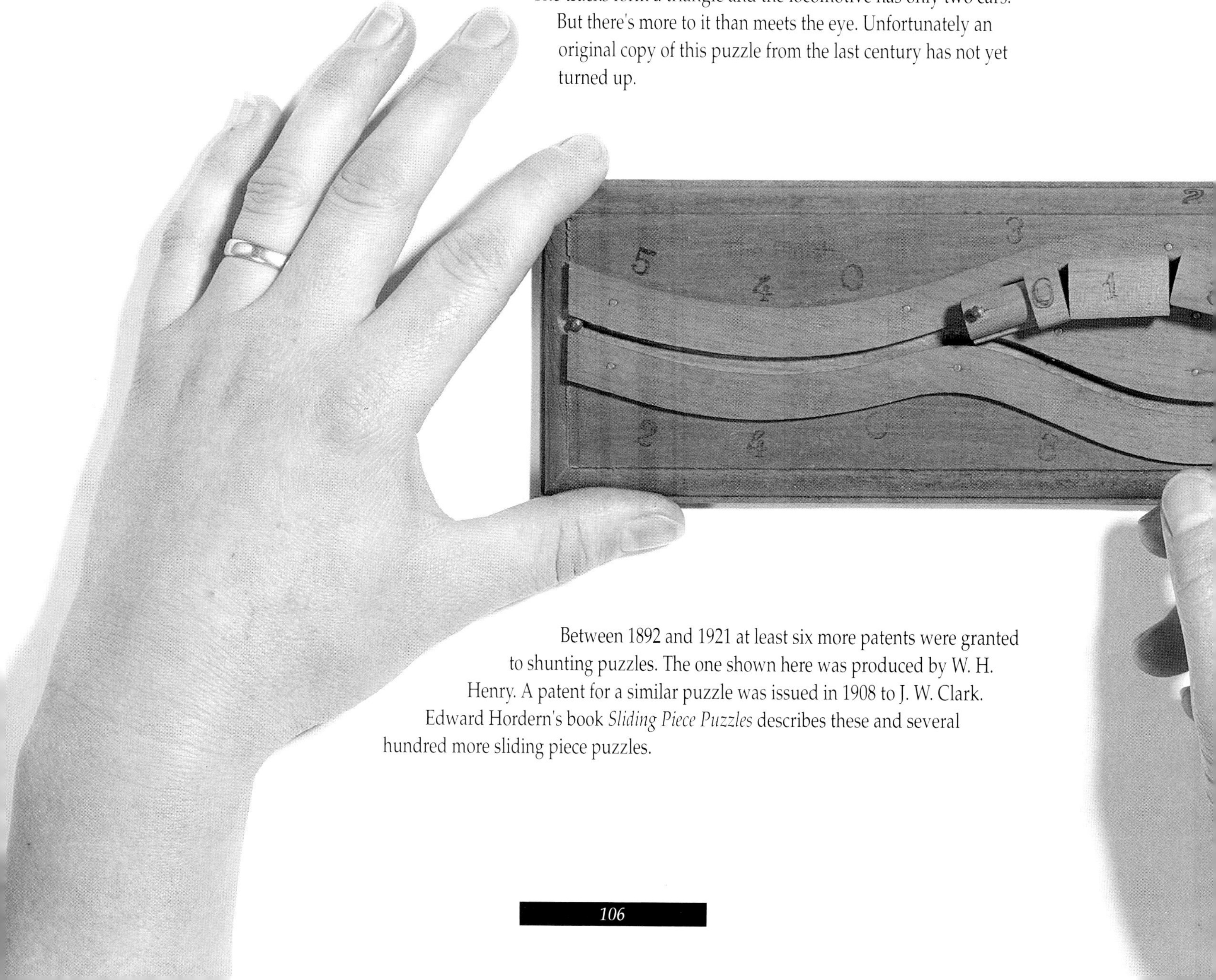

Between 1892 and 1921 at least six more patents were granted to shunting puzzles. The one shown here was produced by W. H. Henry. A patent for a similar puzzle was issued in 1908 to J. W. Clark. Edward Hordern's book *Sliding Piece Puzzles* describes these and several hundred more sliding piece puzzles.

HOW TO MAKE THIS RAILROAD PUZZLE

A 3⅛ x 12 in. (8 x 30 cm) wooden board makes the base. To this are added two layers of 1/16 in. (2 mm) plywood. The diagram gives the shape of these layers. The first layer forms the groove along which the locomotive and the cars move. The moving pieces each have two tacks in them, one in each end, with extra large and flat heads. You can use upholstery tacks, for example. The width of the head must fit in the groove.

The top layer is to prevent the train from being removed from the groove. The width of the groove in this layer is equal to the width of the tack pin. When you have placed the train in the groove, you can keep it from coming out by inserting small nails at the ends.

The locomotive and the cars can be made of 3⁄4 x 3⁄4 in. (2 x 2 cm) and 2 x 5⁄8 in. (5 x 1.5 cm) wooden blocks. It is fun to carve them into a real-looking train and then paint them. Number the pieces 0 through 5. The locomotive is 0 and the cars 1 through 5.

SOLUTION

The manufacturer of this puzzle described the puzzle as follows: From a given position move the pieces in 11 steps to form a different order. The numbers for the moves are given on the puzzle. The whole thing is somewhat obscure, so we propose that you place the pieces in a certain order at one side of the puzzle. You then think up an order in which you want the pieces to end up at the other side. There's an endless variety. The rules are as follows: The locomotive can only go forward and backward. The cars have to be pulled or pushed by the locomotive.

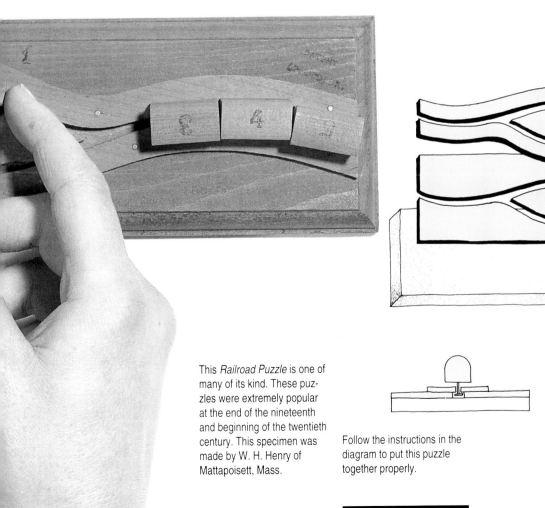

This *Railroad Puzzle* is one of many of its kind. These puzzles were extremely popular at the end of the nineteenth and beginning of the twentieth century. This specimen was made by W. H. Henry of Mattapoisett, Mass.

Follow the instructions in the diagram to put this puzzle together properly.

THE OKLAHOMA PUZZLE

The Oklahoma Puzzle is one of a type of puzzles known as checkerboard-string puzzles. These are puzzles in which a nail has been hammered into each square of a checkerboard pattern. Problems have to be solved using a piece of string. Chess players will be good at such puzzles as the problems are often similar to those encountered in the game of chess.

The Oklahoma Puzzle is a version with 6 x 6 squares and the aim of the puzzle is explained on the back of the board. A U.S.A. inspector went to Oklahoma to check on lot divisions. He took a piece of string and secured it in lot A, then he walked with the string in his hand through all the lots and ended in lot B.

Puzzle inventor Sam Loyd invented a puzzle at the end of the last century consisting of 8 x 8 squares, the so-called Rook's Tour. Loyd described these types of puzzles in his book *Chess Strategy* in 1878. This *Oklahoma Puzzle* is a variation on Loyd's puzzles. Here there are only 6 x 6 squares, but the principle of the puzzle is the same.

However, he was only allowed to walk through each lot once, and was also not allowed to cross through diagonally. He could only walk straight ahead or make an angle of 90° by pulling the string around a nail in the center of a lot. Which route did the inspector take?

HOW TO MAKE AN OKLAHOMA PUZZLE WITH 8 X 8 SQUARES

Take a piece of wood measuring at least 12 x 12 in. (30 x 30 cm), otherwise the puzzle will be difficult to handle and to make. It is advisable to use wood which is between 1/2 and 1 in. (1 and 2.5 cm) thick, so that you can hammer the nails in firmly.

Draw a pattern of 64 squares on the board. In the center of each square you hammer a nail or screw in a screw measuring 1 in. (2.5 cm). Use 32 screws and 32 nails to maintain the chessboard pattern.

Mark the starting points of the five puzzles described here. The location of these points can be found in the solutions at the end of the book.

You can also make a portable version of this puzzle. In that case use thinner wood, smaller nails and make a handle on the board.

PUZZLE PROBLEMS

1. 15-LINE PUZZLE: go from A to B in 15 straight lines. All the nails must be touched. Diagonal lines are forbidden and the lines may not cross each other. The solution can be found at the end of the book.

2. 21-LINE PUZZLE: go from C to D, via all the nails, in 21 straight lines. Diagonal lines are forbidden and the lines may not cross one another.

3. 15-LINE PUZZLE: go from E to F. Touch all the nails and form 15 lines, horizontal, vertical or diagonal. However, the lines may not cross one another.

4. 17-LINE PUZZLE: The nails may only be used as connecting points between the lines. Go from G to H in 17 straight lines. Here the lines may cross one another.

5. 12-LINE PUZZLE: Use only 16 nails to go from J to K in 12 straight lines. The lines may run horizontally, vertically or diagonally, but may not cross one another.

Solutions in Chapter 8.

The pattern of 8 x 8 squares is the basis for five checkerboard puzzles based on the ideas of Sam Loyd at the end of the nineteenth century.

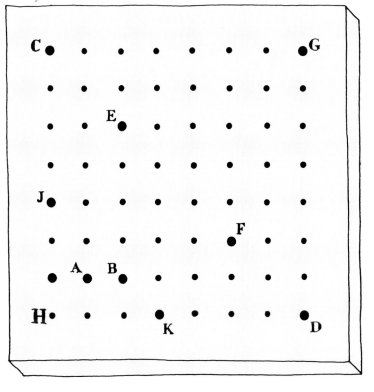

THE YANKEE PUZZLE

At the end of the nineteenth century the strangest puzzles were invented for a strongly expanding market. Puzzles became more and more popular and in order to satisfy the customer, new and increasingly strange and interesting puzzles were invented. The puzzles can be divided into various categories, most of which you have come across in this book.

The puzzle in this photo is one of the so-called maze puzzles. It is a very small pocket-sized puzzle, although I wouldn't put it in my pocket. It mainly consists of nails. This Yankee Puzzle was patented by W. G. Adams on February 11, 1896. It is a board measuring only 2¾ x 2¾ in. (7 x 7 cm), containing 18 tacks. Between these lies a round brass plate with various notches in it. The aim is to twist the plate from nail to nail from the center outwards to one of the edges so that it escapes from the maze.

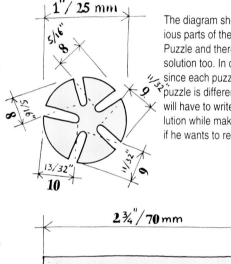

In 1896 W. G. Adams from the Adams & Forbes firm of Philadelphia was granted a patent for his *Yankee Puzzle*, a small puzzle belonging to the maze puzzle category. Despite its small size it is surprisingly difficult to solve.

The diagram shows the various parts of the Yankee Puzzle and thereby the solution too. In other words since each puzzle maker's puzzle is different, the maker will have to write down the solution while making the puzzle if he wants to record it.

HOW TO MAKE THIS YANKEE PUZZLE

SOLUTION

As we have already said, the solution is different for every puzzle. Let someone try it out and you will see how difficult it is.

A piece of plywood measuring 2¾ x 2¾ in. and 3⁄16 in. (7 x 7 cm and 5 mm) thick is most suitable for this puzzle. You also need a round brass (or other metal) disk with a diameter of 1 in. (2.5 cm) and a thickness of 1⁄32 in. (1 mm). And you need 20 tacks with round heads.

Take care: the puzzle which you are about to make is not a copy of the puzzle in the photo but a personal variation. So if you want to remember the solution, you must write it down while you are making the puzzle.

First of all make the notches in the disk. The diagram shows how deep they have to be. Make them about 1⁄16 in. (2 mm) wide. Use a metal saw and a flat file, 1⁄16 in. (1.5 mm) wide. When this is ready, lay the disk in the center of the plywood board. Draw a circle round the disk in this position. Then hammer a nail into the deepest point of one of the notches. After that another nail just in front of the end of another notch. Then slide the disk via that notch around the second nail. Twist the disk a little and hammer a third nail in front of the end of another notch. Continue in this way until the disk can be removed at the side of the board. Now you have to complete the puzzle. Lay the disk back in the center and make blind alleys with the other nails. Be careful that you don't block the good route, or make other routes which are solutions.

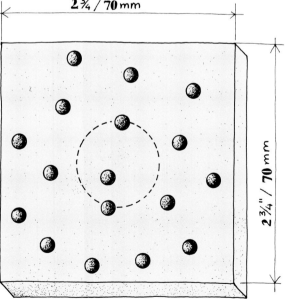

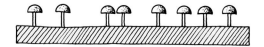

PUZZLES WITH CHECKER PIECES

In Hoffmann's book *Puzzles Old and New* published in 1893, a whole chapter was devoted to puzzles using a checkerboard. It is possible to play all sorts of complicated games and puzzles just using an ordinary set of checkers, that is the board and checkers. Some of these are quite well known.

The adjacent checkerboard shows the positions for such a checker puzzle. The positions are as follows: four white and four black men have been placed alternately. The two empty squares at the top in that row are part of the puzzle. The purpose is to move the men two at a time so that the four black and four white men lie four in a row next to one another. This has to be achieved in four moves. When these moves have been completed the men should lie as follows: from top to bottom, two empty squares, four black and four white men.

The final position should be as follows: from top to bottom, two empty squares, four black and four white men.

This checkerboard dates from 1890 and it features the checker storage panels at the sides of the board which are open at the top and the bottom. There is an 8 x 8 checker board on the back.

THE NEW 15 PUZZLE

Sam Loyd invented an enormous number of puzzles at the end of the last century. Many of them were very successful and you have encountered several of them in this book. But sometimes he falsely took credit for puzzles invented by others. One puzzle Loyd claimed but we are not sure he invented is the 14-15 Puzzle, which came out about 1880. It consisted of a square box with 15 numbered pieces which fitted into a pattern. By sliding the pieces around, the pieces with the numbers 14 and 15 had to change places. This turned out to be impossible. Even so, the puzzle was a success, partly due to a contest offering a $1,000 prize conducted by Sam Loyd. In 1923 the New 15 Puzzle was put on the market. This time it seemed impossible to move the number 15 from the middle to its proper place. However, a solution is possible in 81 moves.

Solution in Chapter 8

HOW TO MAKE THE NEW 15 PUZZLE

Use two pieces of cardboard, 6 x 6 in. (15 x 15 cm) and 15 numbers from a lotto/bingo game. Transfer the diagram onto one of the pieces of cardboard. Cut out the pentagon with the star and glue it onto the other piece of cardboard. Draw circles with the numbers in the grooves, as shown in the diagram.

THE PUZZLE PROBLEM
Lay all the pieces in their marked places, except the 15, which you put in the middle. By sliding one piece at a time, the 15 has to be moved back to its own place. The solution consists of 81 moves! This puzzle seems impossible at first.

The New 15 Puzzle is a new version of the 14-15 Sliding Block Puzzle from the last century. That puzzle was impossible, this one is almost so. This "new" puzzle was invented in 1923 and produced in England.

The famous "impossible" *14-15 Puzzle* by Sam Loyd. Despite the fact that the puzzle couldn't be solved, Sam Loyd helped make it a great success with his $1,000 prize for a solution. No one collected the prize money since a puzzle solution was impossible.

1	2	3	4
5	6	7	8
9	10	11	12
13	15	14	

The inside of the box shows the grooves for the disks and the positions of the numbers.

THE 13 PUZZLE

With the impossible 14-15 Puzzle still fresh in the public's memory, the Columbia Novelty Manufacturing Co. in about 1906 produced the 13 Puzzle. It is also a sliding block puzzle but in this case the pieces, numbered 1 to 13, are placed in the box in random order. By sliding them around you have to try and arrange the numbers 1–12 along the edges in the right order, and number 13 has to be in the middle. Once again not an easy task, but as it says on the box: "it can be done".

The Columbia Novelty Manufacturing Co. of Boston brought out *The 13 Puzzle* in about 1906. It was a variation on the impossible 14-15 Puzzle which appeared in about 1880.

HOW TO MAKE THE 13 PUZZLE

Jerry Slocum made the 13 Puzzle in a compact disk box. He used a plywood frame and 13 disks sawed from a stick. The frame and the triangles which determine the grooves through which the disks slide, are glued onto a piece of cardboard. The whole thing fits into a compact disk box, where it can be kept safe.

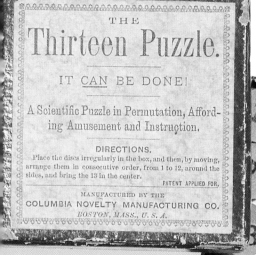

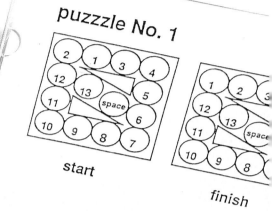

puzzle No. 1

start

finish

puzzle No. 2

start- same as above

finish- consecutive order 1 to 12 clockwise around sides with 13 in original position

This version of *The 13 Puzzle* was made by Jerry Slocum on the occasion of the 11th Puzzle Party in 1991 in Culver City, and given as a souvenir to attendees.

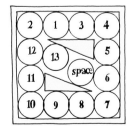

START 1   **FINISH 2**

The starting position (1) and the finishing position (2) of the disks.

SOLUTION

This puzzle is a nice one to solve yourself. Be a sport. Let us know if you succeeded.

NO-JUMP-O

This tin sliding-block puzzle was invented by Lawrence Compton and Howard M. Houck in 1899; they were granted a patent on August 22 of that same year. The puzzle was produced by the Atlantic Mfg. Co. It is a different type of puzzle than the railroad puzzle or the square sliding-block puzzles which we know today. Nineteen counters in different colors, six blue, five white, five red and three with a star are placed in the tin holder in random order. The end result is shown on the lid of the box in which the puzzle is kept: one star at each corner of the triangle and one color on each side. No matter how the pieces are placed in the puzzle to start, this solution can always be achieved. So it will keep you busy for hours.

The diagram shows the exact shape, size and proportions of the puzzle.

The No-Jump-O-Puzzle is exactly what its name implies. No jumps may be made to solve the puzzle. This sliding block puzzle was designed by Lawrence Compton and Howard M. Houck in 1899 and put on the market by the Atlantic Mfg. Co. in that same year.

HOW TO MAKE A NO-JUMP-O

You need:

One panel of plywood, 85/8 x 51/8 in. (22 x 13 cm).

One strip of wood 1/4 x 1/2 in. (0.5 x 1 cm) thick and 61/2 ft. (2 meters) long.

13 disks 7/8 in. (22 mm) in diameter, six disks 27/32 in. (21 mm) diameter and about 1/2 in. (1 cm) thick.

Draw the pattern in the diagram on the panel.

Be careful: it is important that the difference between the blue and the other disks is minimal, otherwise the puzzle won't work properly. The blue disks should fit in the upper-left groove in a zig-zag line.

Now you are going to glue the strips to form the pattern. If you want to be sure that they stay in the right shape, lay the strips of the pattern on the panel. Mount the strips which form the track between which the disks slide with wood glue, or nail them with thin nails. Use short pieces of the strip to close the corners.

A star is painted on three 7/8 in. (22 mm) diameter disks; five 7/8 in. (22 mm) diameter disks are painted red and five with a 7/8 (22 mm) diameter are left blank.

The six disks 27/32 in. (21 mm) are painted blue.

SOLUTION

The successive steps for working out the puzzle are as follows:

1. The disks being indiscriminately placed in the grooves, commence by moving a white disk in the switch.

2. Move the disks around until a star confronts the switch. Then move the star into the switch.

3. Move all the disks around, exept the star and the white disk in the switch until all the white disks by shifting at the switch are in line in the upper right groove, except the one retained in the switch.

4. Now move all the disks, except the star and white disk, in the switch, and by means of the switch arrange all the red disks in the base-groove and all the white disks, except the one in the switch, in the upper right groove.

5. Move all the disks around, except the two in the switch, keeping each series of color together and arrange all the blue disks in the same groove.

6. Now move all the disks, except the two in the switch, around until a star-disk confronts the switch. Then move said star-disk in the switch, thus making two star-disks and a white disk in the switch.

7. Now move the disks until the blue series in the base-groove confront the first star-disk in the switch. Then move one of the star-disks out of the switch ahead of the blue series and move all the disks, except the two in the switch, until the six blue disks occupy the upper left groove in a zigzag line, with a star-disk at either end.

This latter position is the key to the solution of the puzzle. The special construction in this puzzle by which this position is obtainable is that the disks in the blue series having the largest number are slightly smaller in size than the disks in the other series, where the number is smaller. This fact permits the assembling of the disks of the series having the largest number in a groove-space, which will only receive the disks of either of the other series having a smaller number, and thereby make room in the upper left groove adjacent to switch for the passage into the upper-.right groove of the disk that has been retained in the switch. There are no disks now in the switch. At this point we have the blue disks all in the upper-left groove, the red disks in the base-groove and the white disks in

the upper-right groove, and a star disk separating each series.

8. Now move the star disk confronting the switch back into the switch and then continue to move all the disks to the right or from the base-groove along the upper right groove until a star-disk arrives at the angle of the base-and the upper left groove. Then leave the star-disk in the angle between the said grooves.

9. Now move the disks around (leaving the star-disk in the angle between the base and the upper left groove and one star-disk in the switch) until the second star-disk confronts the switch. Then move said star-disk into

the switch. Now move all the colored disks until the red disks in the base groove confront the switch. Then move one of the stars from the switch between the red disks and the white disks. Then move all the disks (except the star-disk in the angle between the base and the upper left groove and one star-disk in the switch) around until the blue disks are lined up in the base-groove and are confronting the switch.

10. Now move the star-disk from the switch to separate the blue and the red disks and the puzzle is solved.

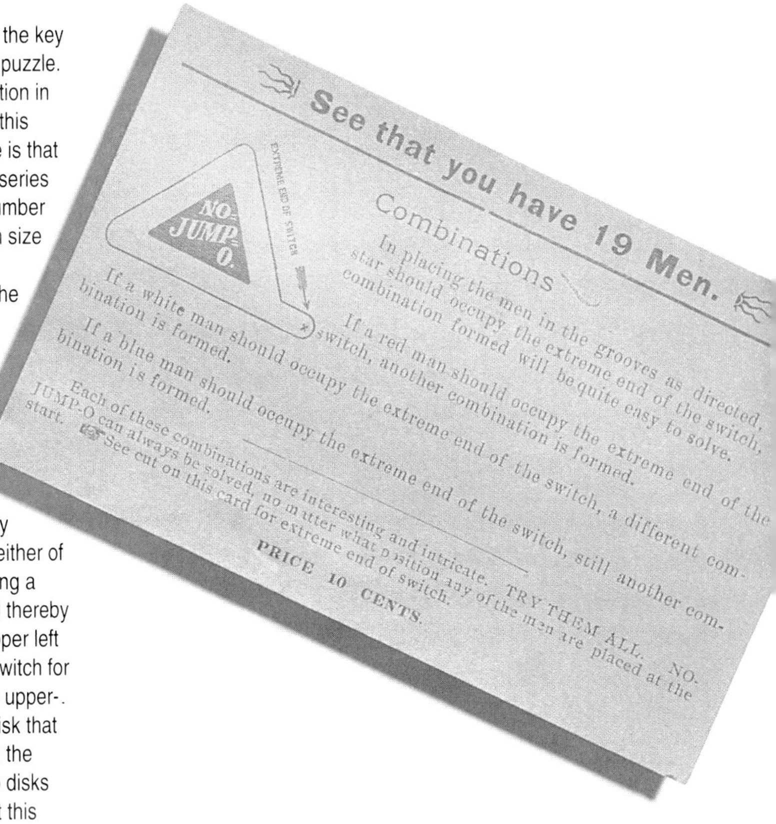

In this special case we tell the solution on this page, because you need the picture of the puzzle while reading the solution. The solution will show you how clever this puzzle is.

See that you have 19 Men.

Combinations

In placing the men in the grooves as directed, star should occupy the extreme end of the switch, combination formed will be quite easy to solve.

If a white man should occupy the extreme end of the switch, another combination is formed.

If a blue man should occupy the extreme end of the switch, still another combination is formed.

Each of these combinations are interesting and intricate. TRY THEM ALL. NO-JUMP-O can always be solved, no matter what position any of the men are placed at the start. ☞ See cut on this card for extreme end of switch.

EXTREME END OF SWITCH

NO JUMP O

PRICE 10 CENTS.

The card gives other puzzle combinations to solve.

FLIP-A-RING

6.

Dexterity puzzles.
Objective: Manual dexterity is
primary to solve the puzzle.
Pages 116–117

Dexterity puzzles have been played all over the world for centuries. Examples exist from pre-Colombian South America (Pommawonga), from Alaska (Gazinta), China and the Middle East. These games were probably meant to train the hand-eye coordination in children, something which they would need later in life when hunting, etc.

The most famous of these games is probably the Cup-and-Ball game. A forerunner of this was played in ancient China, after which it moved via the Middle East to Europe. It is not clear when the game was first played there but we do know that it was very popular in France in the sixteenth, seventeenth and eighteenth centuries. It was called Bilboquet and even the French King Henri III (1586–1589) was an enthusiastic player.

The photo shows two other dexterity games: Flip-a-Ring from 1943 and One-in-the-Eye-for-Kruger. Guess where that one came from!

HOW TO MAKE A BILBOQUET

You need: a ring, a piece of string and a stick with a pointed end. Thread the ring onto the string, the string onto the stick and you have a simple Bilboquet. Or what about a pencil, a piece of string and a pencil sharpener? A more difficult version is a stick with a pointed end, a piece of string and a wooden ball with a hole in it. You have to have good dexterity to solve that one!

Jay Bee Games of New York put this cardboard dexterity game on the market in 1943. Throw the ring over one of the fingers and win as many points as possible.

ONE-IN-THE-EYE-FOR-KRUGER

A different type of dexterity puzzle has a more sadistic background. These are cards whereby you make fun of a person or animal. Of course, these puzzles are extremely suitable for making caricatures of famous people. Pick somebody who is out of favor and make a puzzle centered around this person.
A wonderful example of this is the One-in-the-Eye-for-Kruger puzzle. As a result of the Boer War, Uncle Paul Kruger wasn't too popular in England. This puzzle appeared on the market in about 1900, and the aim was to shoot a bullet attached by an elastic band through Kruger's eye. If you shot the bead exactly into Kruger's left eye and the eye fell out you won two points. If you shot the bead right through the left eye, you won four points. I think the English had a lot of fun with this one.

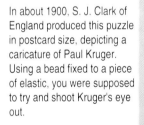

ONE-IN-THE-EYE-FOR-THE-DEVIL?

A drawing of the devil can be put to great use in this puzzle. You glue the drawing on a thick piece of cardboard and cut out the eye, making the hole quite large. You then stick the circle of cardboard with the eye on it to the back of the puzzle with a strip of cloth, so that you don't have to go looking for it when you have shot accurately.
The bullet is made from a bead and a piece of elastic. Tie the end of the elastic to the card. This game is a bit bloodthirsty, but it's fun. Of course you can also use a drawing of a Bullseye target. Just use your imagination.

In about 1900, S. J. Clark of England produced this puzzle in postcard size, depicting a caricature of Paul Kruger. Using a bead fixed to a piece of elastic, you were supposed to try and shoot Kruger's eye out.

THE DEVIL'S FAN. Patented in Germany.

Foreign patents applied for. WHERE'S THE THIRTEENTH DEVIL GONE TO?!!

This Devil's Fan comes from Germany, but the puzzle idea is from Sam Loyd. His puzzle was patented in 1896. This puzzle was an unqualified success; during Loyd's lifetime, more than 10 million copies were sold!

HOW TO MAKE THIS FAN

Long live modern technology! Make a color photocopy of the fan and mount it on a circle of cardboard. Cut an inner circle loose from the outer circle. Use a strip of cardboard as the handle and glue this to the inner circle, so that you can twist the outer circle around. Now you can see how clever Loyd was to think of this puzzle.

THE
DEVIL'S FAN

It is only fair that one of the last puzzles in this book should come from the mind and hands of Sam Loyd. As inventor of many different types of puzzles, he has appeared often in the book and we will include here one of his most successful ideas. In 1896, Loyd was granted a patent for his Get off the Earth Puzzle, an ingenious puzzle whereby one begins with 13 figures and by twisting a disk, only 12 remain! More than 10 million copies of this puzzle were sold during Loyd's lifetime! During the presidential campaign of 1897, the Republican Party distributed the puzzle to advertise their candidate, McKinley.

Sam Loyd made use of an existing puzzle, the line-paradox. You may know of the puzzle in which a number of lines or figures stand in a row; they are cut by a diagonal line. By shifting the two halves of the puzzle, one of the figures disappears. Loyd did the same thing really, but he changed this straight line into a circle whereby creating a much more ingenious puzzle. The figures are drawn in a spiral. A circle has been cut out in the middle, whereby cutting each figure in two in a different place. By turning the central circular piece the various parts of the figures form an extra devil. The last two devils have their feet in the heads of the devils below, but that doesn't really matter.

Loyd's puzzle was immediately used by all sorts of firms for advertising, and many different versions appeared. But whether they were devils, sailors or lions who disappeared and appeared again, the principle remains the same. The example in the photo here uses devils. It is probably best in this case to go from 13 to 12 devils, instead of the other way round. Devils shouldn't really be multiplied if possible, should they? And 13 devils at that!

A MAGIC PLAYING CARD

The magic playing card puzzle is a geometrical paradox. It involves cutting up a shape and rearranging the pieces. This gives away the solution, but the idea is so attractive that even if you know the solution, it remains a nice puzzle. The paradox of a disappearing part of a puzzle is very old. The book *Rational Recreations* by William Hooper, published in 1794, included a description of the paradox in The Geometric Money. With this type of puzzle– in fact The Devil's Fan is one of these too– it seems as though a part disappears. In the case of this playing card you have to lay the pieces face down first and then, using the back of the card, assemble the puzzle. The next step is to turn the pieces over and assemble the puzzle from the front. And. . . there really is a piece missing on the front side but not on the back.

HOW TO MAKE THIS PUZZLE CARD

First of all make a color copy of this page (the publisher is not too pleased about this, but never mind). Then glue the front to a piece of cardboard and cut out the pieces. Remove the piece which is to form the hole. Turn the pieces over and lay them down in such a way that no hole is visible. Glue down the rear side and cut out the pieces again.

In the *Libro Primo d'Architettura* by the Italian Sebastiano Serlio, published about 1537, a geometric paradox was shown when a 3 x 10 board was cut on a diagonal and slid to form a 4 x 7 table with a 3 x 1 piece left over. However, Serlio didn't notice the area change. Likewise your friends may have trouble explaining the missing piece on the front of *The Magic Playing Card Puzzle*.

THE ARROW THROUGH THE BOTTLE

In our last book we published an illustration of a Coke bottle which was pierced by a wooden arrow. That book appeared in 1986 and still nobody has sent us the solution.
So we try again. Who knows how the arrow went through the bottle? We are very curious to know if anyone has found the solution. We know it, really! But we hope that someone else is clever enough to find the answer.
We thought this would be a nice way to end a puzzle book in which most of the solutions are included. But we are not giving away this one! Sweet dreams.

Solution **not** in Chapter 8.

Gary Foshee of Seattle made this puzzle in 1979. Since then few people have been able to find the solution.

Solutions

Strictly in case of desperate need

Pages 8-9 **Tangrams**

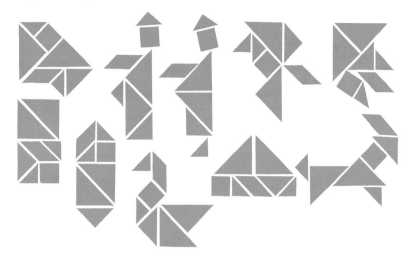

Pages 12-13 **Letter Puzzles**

The F-D Puzzle:

The New L-Square Puzzle

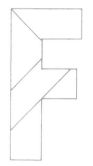

Squares & Oblongs Puzzle

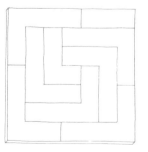

Page 14 **Square Dissection Puzzles**

Pages 20–21 **Animal Puzzles**
The principle of all the puzzles is shown in the diagram.

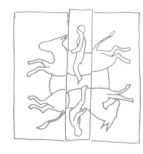

Pages 18-19 **Magic Squares** *The Giant Puzzle*
R=red, B=blue, P=pink, Y=yellow, G=green.

R1	B3	P5	Y7	G9
Y7	G9	R1	B3	P5
B3	P5	Y7	G9	R1
G9	R1	B3	P5	Y7
P5	Y7	G9	R1	B3

Pages 26–27 **A Puzzle Made Using Nuts**
The Hexagone

Page 28 **Magic Numbers**
The Washington Monument Puzzle
Solutions by Dick Hess

60	95	30	25	60	95	30	25
55	25	20	70	55	25	20	70
55	10	20	50	55	10	20	50
15	45	55	65	15	45	55	65
90	55	90	80	55	90	80	90
55	60	90	85	60	90	85	55
55	45	95	15	55	45	95	15
55	75	65	55	75	65	55	55
55	70	35	55	70	35	55	55
60	75	55	55	55	55	60	75

60	95	30	25	60	95	30	25
55	25	20	70	55	25	20	70
55	10	20	50	55	10	20	50
45	55	65	15	55	65	15	45
90	55	90	80	55	90	80	90
60	90	85	55	55	60	90	85
15	55	45	95	55	45	95	15
65	55	55	75	55	55	75	65
55	55	70	35	55	55	70	35
55	60	75	55	55	55	60	75

60	95	30	25	60	95	30	25
55	25	20	70	55	25	20	70
10	20	50	55	10	20	50	55
15	45	55	65	55	65	15	45
55	90	80	90	90	80	90	55
60	90	85	55	55	60	90	85
95	15	55	45	55	45	95	15
75	65	55	55	65	55	55	75
55	55	70	35	35	55	55	70
75	55	55	60	75	55	55	60

60	95	30	25	60	95	30	25
25	20	70	55	25	20	70	55
50	55	10	20	50	55	10	20
65	15	45	55	45	55	65	15
55	90	80	90	90	55	90	80
55	60	90	85	85	55	60	90
95	15	55	45	15	55	45	95
55	75	65	55	55	55	75	65
35	55	55	70	70	35	55	55
60	75	55	55	60	75	55	55

60	95	30	25
20	70	55	25
55	10	20	50
15	45	55	65
90	55	90	80
85	55	60	90
55	45	95	15
65	55	55	75
55	70	35	55
55	55	60	75

Dick Hess wrote a computer program to find these solutions. "If I programmed correctly that should be all there are." Dick said.

Page 82 The Braided Leather Puzzle

The diagram shows the braiding of the leather strip.

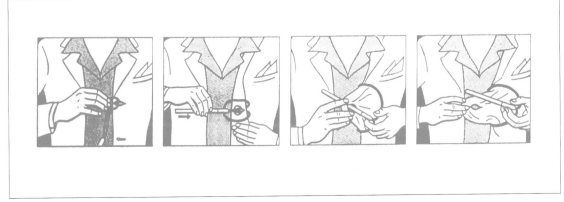

Pages 36–37 Matchstick Puzzles

From top to bottom

Pages 96–97 The Indians and Travellers Puzzle

Indians and Travellers Puzzle 1
I = Indian W = White

I+W>
W<
2I>
I<
2W>
W+I<
2W>
I<
2I>
I<
2I>

Indians and Travellers Puzzle 2

I+W<
2W>
I<
2I>
I<

The Jealous Husbands 3
A,B, C are women, AH, BH, CH are husbands

A+AH>
AH<
B+C>
A<
BH+CH>
C+CH<
AH+CH<
B<
B+C>
AH<
A+AH>

The Fox, Goose and Corn Puzzle 4
M = man, F = fox, C = corn, G = goose

M + G >
M <
M + C >
M + G <
M + F >
M <
M + G >

The Men and Boys Puzzle 5
M = man, 100 k., B = boy, 50 k.

2 B >
1 B <
1 M >
1 B <
2 B >
1 B <
1 M >
1 B <
2 B >

Pages 78–79 Magic Holetite Pencil

This is the original solution enclosed with the puzzle.

Page 98 Double Five Puzzle

7 > 10, 5 > 2, 9 >4, 3 > 6, 1 > 8,

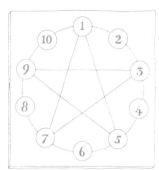

Page 99 The Great 13 Puzzle

3 >7, 13 > 3, 11 >13, 2 > 12, 13> 7, 4 > 10, 1 > 11 >
13 > 7, 9 > 5, 3 > 7.
(Solution by Edward Hordern.)

3 >7, 9 > 5, 13 > 3, 11.> 13, 1 >6, 3>7, 2 > 12, 13 > 7, 4 > 10, 11 > 13, 13 > 7.

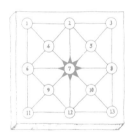

Pages 100-101 Solitaire

15 > C; 9 > 16; 13 > 11; 16 > 9; 7 > 11; 10 > 12; 5 > 7; 4 > 9; 7 > 11; 12 > 10; 27 > 16; C > 15; 14 > 16; 32 > 30; 16 > 27; 17 > 4; 1 > 3; 10 > 2; 20 > 1; 1 > 3; 4 > 17; 22 > 30; 25 > 29; 29 > 31; 26 > 30; 31 > 29; 18 > C; C > 28; 24 > 22; 21 > 29; 28 > C.

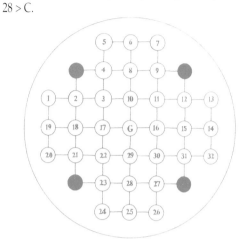

Pages 108-109 The Oklahoma Puzzle

15 Line Puzzle   *17 Line Puzzle*

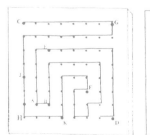

21 Line Puzzle   *12 Line Puzzle*

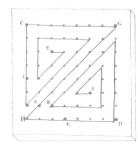

15 Line Puzzle

Page 102-103 The Triangle Puzzle Board

16 > 8; 4 > 13; 6 > 8; 9 > 7; 3 > 8; 12 > 5; 10 > 16; 15 > 6; 1 > 3; 3 > 8; 13 > 4; 6 > 8; 4 > 13; 16 > 8.

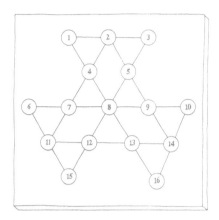

Page 111 Puzzles with Checker Pieces

We number the row of squares from bottom to top from 1 to 10. Now make the following moves:

2 + 3 > 9 + 10
5 + 6 > 2 + 3
8 + 9 > 5 + 6
1 + 2 > 8 + 9

Page 112 The New 15 Puzzle

See the picture on page 112. Pieces may only be slid from circle to circle.

14 >13 > 12 > 11 >15.> 6 > 7 >8 > 9 > 10 > 15 > 6 > 1 > 14 > 13 > 12 > 11 > 6 > 1 > 14 > 13 > 12 > 11 > 6 > 1 > 15 > 10 > 9 > 8 > 7 > 5 > 4 > 3 > 2 > 13 > 12 > 11 > 6 > 1 > 15 > 14 > 12 > 13 > 2 > 3 > 4 > 5 > 12 > 13 > 11 > 6 > 1 > 15 > 14 > 13 > 11 > 6 > 1 > 15 > 14 > 13 > 11 > 12 > 7 > 8 > 9 > 10 > 11 > 12 > 6 > 1 > 15 > 14 > 13 > 12 > 11 > 10 > 9 > 8 > 7 > 6.

Page 120 The Arrow through the Bottle.

As we told you on page 120, we do **not** give the solution.

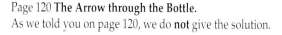

Pages 104-105 **The Pyramids Puzzle**
The picture shows the original enclosed solution of The
Pyramids Puzzle.

▲▲▲

⋯and the prophet Brahma said unto his priests:"⋯By the time you

▲▲▲

FROM time immemorable man has pondered over the mystery of the Pyramids of Egypt. The mathematical interpretation of the dimensions of these pyramids has led many learned students to believe that the ancient Egyptians had a deeper knowledge than exists today of the laws governing the vast network of our universe. It is known that far deeper meaning than the multiplication or division of numbers was discovered in mathematics by the ancient Egyptians. And the interpretation of these mathematical discoveries in relation to the workings of the Universe are believed to be embodied in the construction of the great pyramids which still rest on the sands of the Sahara Desert.

Our most learned students of the present day eagerly grasp and attempt to analyze even the slightest vestige of this mystery which has survived the ages.

It is within the bounds of possibility that the problem which you are about to solve bears some relation to the mathematical interpretations evolved by the ancient Egyptians. It is a simplified version of a problem which has survived the ages and was conceived by the prophet Brahma who lived many centuries ago.

The original problem consisted of three pyramids arranged to form a triangle. Upon the left pyramid, 64 golden discs lay. The problem involves transferring these 64 discs from the left to the right pyramid—transposing one disc at a time only—and putting it either on a vacant pyramid or a larger disc. The vast labor involved in completing this transposition may be realized when we quote the words (in part) of Brahma to his priests: "——by the time you have executed this task, the end of the world will be near!":

By reducing the number of discs from 64 to 8 we have simplified the problem so that it can be solved in a very short time.

Although there are but eight discs to be transposed from the left pyramid to the right pyramid, 255 moves are necessary before the complete transposition of the eight discs is accomplished. This astounding total is reached due to the fact that after each disc has been transferred, the number of moves to transpose each succeeding disc is double the

total moves required to transpose the preceding disc. The ancient Egyptians obtained a complete transposition as follows:
(For reference it will be desirable to distinguish the discs by numbers, the smallest one No. 1, the next larger 2, and so on, up to the largest which will be No. 8.)

CENTER

LEFT

RIGHT

The *three pyramids* we will assume to be placed in a row before us, distinguished by the letters—L, C, R, respectively, equivalent to LEFT, CENTER, RIGHT. The discs are arranged at the outset in proper order—No. 1 uppermost, and so on. We then proceed with the moves as follows:

(1) — 1 on C: (2) — 2 on R: (3) — 1 on R:

We have now transferred two of the rings, and it will be observed that it has taken THREE moves to do it. One might conclude that it will only require eight times three moves to transfer all eight discs. Such is not the case, however, for before each succeeding disc can be brought to the base of the new heap, a constantly increasing number of transpositions will be necessary.

We proceed:
(4) — 3 on C: (6) — 2 on C: (7) — 1 on C:
(5) — 1 on L:

We have now transferred THREE of the discs.

(8) — 4 on R:	(11) — 1 on L:	(14) — 2 on R:
(9) — 1 on R:	(12) — 3 on R:	(15) — 1 on R:
(10) — 2 on L:	(13) — 1 on C:	

FOUR discs are now transferred.

(16) — 5 on C:	(21) — 1 on R:	(27) — 1 on R:
(17) — 1 on L:	(22) — 2 on C:	(28) — 3 on C:
(18) — 2 on C:	(23) — 1 on C:	(29) — 1 on L:
(19) — 1 on C:	(24) — 4 on C:	(30) — 2 on L:
(20) — 3 on L:	(25) — 1 on C:	(31) — 1 on C:
	(26) — 2 on R:	

FIVE discs are now transferred, and it has taken 31 moves to accomplish this.

(32) — 6 on R:	(42) — 2 on C:	(53) — 1 on L:
(33) — 1 on R:	(43) — 1 on C:	(54) — 2 on L:
(34) — 2 on L:	(44) — 3 on L:	(55) — 1 on R:
(35) — 1 on L:	(45) — 1 on R:	(56) — 4 on R:
(36) — 3 on R:	(46) — 2 on L:	(57) — 1 on R:
(37) — 1 on C:	(47) — 1 on L:	(58) — 2 on L:
(38) — 2 on R:	(48) — 5 on R:	(59) — 1 on L:
(39) — 1 on R:	(49) — 1 on C:	(60) — 3 on R:
(40) — 4 on L:	(50) — 2 on R:	(61) — 1 on C:
(41) — 1 on L:	(51) — 1 on R:	(62) — 2 on R:
	(52) — 3 on C:	(63) — 1 on R:

SIX discs are now transferred.

(64) — 7 on C:	(82) — 2 on L:	(100) — 3 on C:
(65) — 1 on L:	(83) — 1 on C:	(101) — 1 on L:
(66) — 2 on C:	(84) — 3 on R:	(102) — 2 on C:
(67) — 1 on C:	(85) — 1 on C:	(103) — 1 on C:
(68) — 3 on L:	(86) — 2 on R:	(104) — 4 on R:
(69) — 1 on R:	(87) — 1 on R:	(105) — 1 on R:
(70) — 2 on L:	(88) — 4 on L:	(106) — 2 on L:
(71) — 1 on L:	(89) — 1 on L:	(107) — 1 on L:
(72) — 4 on C:	(90) — 2 on C:	(108) — 3 on C:
(73) — 1 on C:	(91) — 1 on C:	(109) — 1 on C:
(74) — 2 on R:	(92) — 3 on L:	(110) — 2 on R:
(75) — 1 on R:	(93) — 1 on R:	(111) — 1 on R:
(76) — 3 on C:	(94) — 2 on L:	(112) — 5 on C:
(77) — 1 on L:	(95) — 1 on L:	(113) — 1 on L:
(78) — 2 on C:	(96) — 6 on C:	(114) — 2 on C:
(79) — 1 on C:	(97) — 1 on L:	(115) — 1 on C:
(80) — 5 on L:	(98) — 2 on R:	(116) — 3 on L:
(81) — 1 on R:	(99) — 1 on R:	(117) — 1 on L:

▲▲▲

have transferred these discs, the end of the World will be near⋯⋯"!

▲▲▲

▲ **PYRAMIDS** ▲   ▲ **PYRAMIDS** ▲
▲▲

(118) — 2 on L:	(121) — 1 on C:	(125) — 1 on L:
(119) — 1 on L:	(122) — 2 on R:	(126) — 2 on C:
(120) — 4 on C:	(123) — 1 on R:	(127) — 1 on C:
	(124) — 3 on C:	

SEVEN discs have now been transferred. We have made 127 moves and have, as a matter of fact, completed just HALF of our task. Proceed—

(128) — 8 on R:	(166) — 2 on L:	(204) — 3 on R:
(129) — 1 on R:	(167) — 1 on L:	(205) — 1 on C:
(130) — 2 on L:	(168) — 4 on C:	(206) — 2 on R:
(131) — 1 on L:	(169) — 1 on C:	(207) — 1 on R:
(132) — 3 on R:	(170) — 2 on R:	(208) — 5 on C:
(133) — 1 on C:	(171) — 1 on R:	(206) — 2 on R:
(134) — 2 on R:	(172) — 3 on C:	(207) — 1 on R:
(135) — 1 on R:	(173) — 1 on C:	(208) — 5 on C:
(136) — 4 on L:	(174) — 1 on L:	(209) — 1 on L:
(137) — 1 on L:	(175) — 1 on C:	(210) — 2 on C:
(138) — 2 on C:	(176) — 5 on L:	(211) — 1 on C:
(139) — 1 on C:	(177) — 1 on R:	(212) — 3 on L:
(140) — 3 on L:	(178) — 2 on C:	(213) — 1 on R:
(141) — 1 on R:	(179) — 1 on L:	(214) — 2 on L:
(142) — 2 on L:	(180) — 3 on R:	(215) — 1 on L:
(143) — 1 on L:	(181) — 1 on C:	(216) — 4 on C:
(144) — 5 on R:	(182) — 2 on R:	(217) — 1 on C:
(145) — 1 on C:	(183) — 1 on R:	(218) — 2 on R:
(146) — 2 on R:	(184) — 4 on L:	(219) — 1 on R:
(147) — 1 on R:	(185) — 1 on L:	(220) — 3 on C:
(148) — 3 on C:	(186) — 2 on C:	(221) — 1 on L:
(149) — 1 on L:	(187) — 1 on C:	(222) — 2 on C:
(150) — 2 on C:	(188) — 3 on L:	(223) — 1 on C:
(151) — 1 on C:	(189) — 1 on R:	(224) — 6 on R:
(152) — 4 on R:	(190) — 2 on L:	(225) — 1 on R:
(153) — 1 on R:	(191) — 1 on L:	(226) — 2 on L:
(154) — 2 on L:	(192) — 7 on R:	(227) — 1 on L:
(155) — 1 on L:	(193) — 1 on C:	(228) — 3 on R:
(156) — 3 on R:	(194) — 2 on R:	(229) — 1 on C:
(157) — 1 on C:	(195) — 1 on R:	(230) — 2 on R:
(158) — 2 on R:	(196) — 3 on C:	(231) — 1 on R:
(159) — 1 on R:	(197) — 1 on L:	(232) — 4 on L:
(160) — 6 on L:	(198) — 2 on C:	(233) — 1 on L:
(161) — 1 on L:	(199) — 1 on C:	(234) — 2 on C:
(162) — 2 on C:	(200) — 4 on C:	(235) — 1 on C:
(163) — 1 on C:	(201) — 1 on R:	(236) — 3 on L:
(164) — 3 on L:	(202) — 2 on L:	(237) — 1 on R:
(165) — 1 on R:	(203) — 1 on L:	(238) — 2 on L:

(239) — 1 on L:	(245) — 1 on L:	(250) — 2 on L:
(240) — 5 on R:	(246) — 2 on C:	(251) — 1 on L:
(241) — 1 on C:	(247) — 1 on C:	(252) — 3 on R:
(242) — 2 on R:	(248) — 4 on R:	(253) — 1 on C:
(243) — 1 on R:	(249) — 1 on R:	(254) — 2 on R:
(244) — 3 on C:		(255) — 1 on R:

And thus we have transferred, in 255 moves, 8 of the 64 discs which Brahma instructed his priests to transpose from one pyramid to another, with the admonition, *"By the time you have executed this task, the end of the world will be near!"*

As you may now realize, the 255 moves which you have just completed are but an infinitesimal part of those required to transpose the original 64 discs of this fascinating problem. Some idea of the endless task involved may be gained by comparison with the ancient "Chess-Board" problem. In that problem, one grain of corn was placed on the first square, 2 on the second, 4 on the third, and so on throughout the 64 squares. The total number of grains necessary for the last square amounts to 18,446,774,073,709,551,615! When we realize that the counting of a single billion at the rate of 100 a minute would take 19,024 years, the vast time allotted to the completion of the problem may be comprehended.

Yet the transposition of the 64 golden discs from one pyramid to the other would require an even greater period of time than the completion of the "Chess-Board" problem!

And so, when we transfer—in 255 moves—our 8 discs, we might indeed say that we have "touched upon infinity."

CORRECTION NOTE
MOVE NUMBER 106 SHOULD BE 2 ON L
MOVES NUMBER 206-207-208 ARE DUPLICATED AS A GROUP
ELIMINATE ONE OF THE GROUPS.

The
Solution of
PYRAMIDS

A PROBLEM FROM THE ANCIENTS

▲▲▲

A Problem From The Ancients   *A Problem From The Ancients*

INDEX

Acknowledgments

We would like to thank puzzle designers, makers, and solvers from all over the world that have contributed generously to this book. Some of the designers we know well, some are known by their patents, and some are unknown. The puzzle designers and makers that we especially thank include: Stewart Coffin, Jean-Claude Constantin, Bill Cutler, Mike Duffy, Gary Foshee, Hikimi Puzzles, Robert Jackson, David Klarner, Matti Linkola, Sam Loyd, Charlie Miaorana, Jerry McFarland, Julius Pavlovic, Jim Riley, Corky Storer, Wil Strijbos, Toyo Glass Co., Michael Weber, Vernon Wood and Nob Yoshigahara.

We also thank for their generous contributions of solutions, historical information, and help in obtaining the puzzles shown in this book: Martin Gardner, Dieter Gebhardt, Dick Hess, Edward Hordern, Anatoly Kalinin, Angelo Lewis, David Singmaster and his incredibly valuable 'Sources', and Nob Yoshigahara.

References

Ball, W.W. Rouse, Revised by H.S.M. Coxeter, *Mathematical Recreations and Essays*. Macmillan & Co., London, 11th ed., 1939, 418pp., hardbound.

Beasley, John D. *The Ins and Outs of Peg Solitaire*. Oxford University Press, Oxford, 1985, 275pp., hardbound.

Bestelmeier, Georg Hieronimus. *Bestelmeier Katalog*. Magazin Von Verschiedenen Kunst und Abbildungen. Edition Olms, Zürich (Nurnberg 1803), 1979, hardbound. (German).

Coffin, Stewart T. *Puzzle Craft*. Stewart T. Coffin, Lincoln, Mass., 1985, 98pp., paperback.

Coffin, Stewart T. *The Puzzling World of Polyhedral Dissection*. Oxford University Press, Oxford, 1990, 196pp., hardbound.

Filipiak, Anthony S. *100 Puzzles How to Make and How to Solve Them*. A.S. Barnes & Co., N.Y., 1942, 120pp, hardbound. (Reprinted as *Mathematical Puzzles And Other Brain Teasers* by Bell Publishing Co., N.Y.)

Hoffmann, Professor A. Lewis. *Puzzles Old And New*. Frederick Warne & Co., London, 1893, 394pp., hardbound.

Hooper, W. *Rational Recreations*. B. Low and Son; and G.G. and J. Robinson, London, 1794, vol. IV, 367pp, hardbound.

Hordem, Edward. *Sliding Piece Puzzles*. Oxford University Press, Oxford, 1986, 249pp., hardbound.

Loyd, Sam. *The 8th Book of Tan*, Part I. Loyd & Co., New York, 1903, 32pp.,paperback. (Reprinted by Dover, New York, 1968, 52pp., paperback.)

Loyd, Sam II (editor). *Cyclopedia Of Puzzles*. Lamb Publishing Co., New York, 1914, 384pp., hardbound.; (Reprinted by Pinnacle Books, New York, 1976).

Ozanam, Jaques. *Récréations Mathématiques et physiques*. Chez Claude Jombert, Paris, 1735, vol. IV, 446pp., hardbound. (French).

Slocum, Jerry and Jack Botermans. *Puzzles Old and New*. University of Washington Press, Seattle, Wa., 1986, 160pp., hardbound.

Slocum, Jerry. *Making and Solving Puzzles*. Science and Mechanics Magazine, vol. 26, no.5, Oct. 1955 (pp. 121-126); Also *Magic Handbook*, (pp107-112). Science and Mechanics Publishing Co., Chicago, Ill., 1961, 153pp., paperback.

Van Delft, Pieter and Jack Botermans. *Creative Puzzles of the World*. Harry N. Abrams, New York, 1978, 200pp., hardbound.

Wyatt, Edwin M., *Puzzles in Wood*. Bruce Publishing Co., Milwaukee, Wisc., 1928, 64pp., paperback.; Reprinted by Woodcraft Supply Corp., Woodburn, Mass., 1980.

Wyatt, Edwin M., *Wonders In Wood*, Bruce Publishing Co., Milwaukee, Wisc., 1946, 76pp., paperback.